FAST START

Getting Ready to Read

A Research-Based, Send-Home Literacy
Program With 60 Reproducible Poems
and Activities That Ensure
Reading Success for Every Child

• • • • • • • • • • • •

Nancy Padak and Timothy V. Rasinski

SCHOLASTIC

New York • Toronto • London • Auckland • Sydney
Mexico City • New Delhi • Hong Kong • Buenos Aires

Dedication

For parents and teachers, for the support you provide in helping young children take their first steps toward literacy.

Acknowledgments

The folks at Scholastic have been enthusiastic supporters of Fast Start, and we thank them—especially Joanna Davis-Swing, Terry Cooper, and Virginia Dooley.

Cover design: Brian LaRossa
Interior design: LDL Designs
Interior illustrations: pages 42 and 56: Paige Billin-Frye;
pages 70, 94, 100, 106, 108, 110, 124, 140, 142: Dana Regan;
page 82: Steve Cox; pages 128 and 130: James Graham Hale;
page 134: Sue Dennen; all other illustrations by Maxie Chambliss

ISBN-13: 978-0-545-03179-0
ISBN-10: 0-545-03179-6
Copyright © 2008 by Nancy Padak and Timothy V. Rasinski
Published by Scholastic Inc.
All rights reserved.
Printed in the U.S.A.

2 3 4 5 6 7 8 9 10 40 15 14 13 12 11 10 09

Contents

Welcome to Fast Start!

Learning to read is one of the most important accomplishments of early childhood. Success in reading leads to success in other areas of school and throughout life. And research has convinced us that children's families have an important role to play in their growth as readers (Henderson & Berla, 1994; U.S. Department of Education, 1994). That's why we developed Fast Start, a simple and engaging way for children to take their initial steps toward literacy both in school and at home.

The original version of Fast Start, described in *Fast Start for Early Learners* (also available from Scholastic, 2005), is intended for parents and children in grades K-2. Its success led to this version, which is designed for younger children. Most of the poems collected here are familiar Mother Goose rhymes. The companion activities focus on helping children learn about print, including letter names and sounds and one-to-one correspondence. We also include some simple and fun phonemic awareness activities, such as rhyming games. Although we envisioned the program for 4- and 5-year-olds, older children with special needs may also benefit from the program.

Fast Start: Getting Ready to Read differs from its predecessor in one major way: Poems in this version are accompanied by two sets of activities, one for use in preschool or kindergarten classrooms and the other for use by parents or caregivers at home. Working with the same poems in school and at home fosters success and allows children to develop the familiarity with text that serves as an important foundation for learning about print. As adults help children listen to and try to read the poems, children will become familiar with some classic children's poetry. They will also gain important insight into how print works, which will prepare them effectively for their future efforts at learning to read.

The repeated listening and reading that is part of the Fast Start routine may help some young children begin learning to read. Most, however, will simply enjoy the poems and learn about some critical print concepts. Children's success with these activities will help them develop positive attitudes toward reading and themselves as readers. Activity that is focused, intensive, engaging, and authentic will give many children a "Fast Start" in reading, and that's what this program is all about.

Enjoy!

Research-Based, Research-Proven

Fast Start is based on fundamental principles of effective fluency instruction (Rasinski & Hoffman, 2003). We have implemented Fast Start in a number of settings; results have been remarkably and universally positive:

✳ A 5-week pilot implementation with struggling readers in a university summer reading clinic yielded strong correlations between parent participation and various measures of reading achievement for struggling readers in the primary through middle grades (Rasinski, 1995).

✻ An 11-week, experimental study with beginning first graders found that students considered most at risk in reading (as measured by the pretest) grew the most on measures of letter and word recognition and reading fluency. In fact, the struggling first graders who participated in Fast Start made approximately twice the progress in letter and word recognition and fluency (correct words read per minute in reading a grade-appropriate passage) than students in the control group (Rasinski & Stevenson, 2005).

✻ We worked with K–1 teachers in a 2-year implementation of Fast Start in 18 elementary schools in an urban school district. Results indicated that kindergarten children who were involved in Fast Start had significantly greater word vocabulary growth, attained concepts about print more quickly, and learned to identify uppercase and lowercase letters more quickly than students who did not participate in Fast Start. Using measures of authentic reading, we found that first-grade students who were at least somewhat involved in the program significantly outperformed their peers who were not involved. In addition, analysis of surveys and interviews showed that Fast Start participants, both children and their parents or caregivers, were overwhelmingly positive about the experience (Padak & Rasinski, 2004, 2006).

Fast Start: Getting Ready to Read is designed for use at home as well as at school. In fact, all of the research cited above involved home use. The theory and research supporting the inclusion of parents in children's education, especially in the early years of school, is deep and compelling (Chavkin, 1993; Durkin, 1966; Epstein, 1989, 1991; Henderson, 1988; Henderson & Berla, 1994; Neidermeyer, 1970; Postlethwaite & Ross, 1992; Pressley, 2002; Rasinski, 1989, 2003; U.S. Department of Education, 1994). Both the focus of the program and its use in homes, then, have a very strong research base.

The Fast Start Program: Poems and Activity Pages

The Fast Start routine is simple. For 5 to 10 minutes each day, both in school and at home, adults read short poems to children and then engage them in developmentally appropriate skill-building activities. The school and home activities complement each other. For example, at school, children may be developing awareness of a word family found in a poem, while at home they may be practicing awareness of this word family by clapping or raising their hands as they hear words from this word family. Moreover, you will see that each Mother Goose poem has a "partner"—a related version that repeats the sounds, words, and/or word families found in the original. This repetition supports children's learning and fosters their success.

THE POEM PAGES

The 60 poems in the program have been selected for early readers. There are enough poems to use in school and to copy for use at home for the better part of a school year. We recommend that children, teachers, and parents or caregivers work with one or two poems per week. After you have introduced the program to parents, ask them to spend five minutes or so with a poem and activities each evening.

Many of the poems are familiar Mother Goose rhymes. For each traditional verse, we have written a new poem that repeats sounds, words, or word families. For example:

> ### Play Days (original)
> *How many days has my baby to play?*
> *Saturday, Sunday, Monday,*
> *Tuesday, Wednesday, Thursday, Friday,*
> *Saturday, Sunday, Monday.*

> ### Ways to Play (new poem)
> *How many ways has my baby to play?*
> *Trucks and toys for girls and boys*
> *Dolls and games for them, too.*
> *How many ways has my baby to play?*
> *More than just a few.*

These new poems add variety, yet continue to reinforce concepts students have been working on. This extended practice gives young students the support they need to develop their early reading skills.

The adult-child reading has several purposes. Adults model fluent and effective reading and provide support for children's efforts. For some children, this repeated reading will lead to sight-word acquisition and learning to read.

THE ACTIVITY PAGES

After an adult has read the poem fluently a few times and invited the children to read along, it's time to move on to the activity pages. The school activities can be conducted

---

2

Ways to Play

How many ways
has my baby to play?
Trucks and toys
for girls and boys.
Dolls and balls
for them, too.
How many ways
has my baby to play?
More than just a few.

26   Fast Start for Early Readers

✻ 2. Ways to Play

ACTIVITIES FOR SCHOOL

❋ Display the poem. Write "play" on the board or chart paper. Ask children to find the word *play* in the poem. Circle this word for them.

❋ Play a riddle game with children. Tell them that the answers will rhyme with (sound like) *play* and that you will give them the beginning sound of the answer.

   1. This is what we do when we buy something. It starts with /p/. (*pay*)

   2. This is what we feed horses. It starts with /h/. (*hay*)

   3. This is a month in spring. It starts with /m/. (*May*)

❋ On a sheet of chart paper write *ay*. Tell children that this combination of letters makes the sound /ay/. Ask them to help make a list of words that have *ay* in them (such as *day, say, play, my,* and *hay*). Record the words on chart paper, and practice reading them with children several times over the next few days. Have students write one or two of the words on paper or whiteboards.

ACTIVITIES FOR HOME

❋ Read the poem aloud. Show your child the first word in the first line of the poem. Ask your child to find the first words of the other lines in the poem.

❋ After reading the poem aloud, write a lowercase and an uppercase *a* on a slip of paper. Show the letters to your child and name them: "This is an uppercase *A*. This is a lowercase *a*." Ask your child to find the letter *a* in the poem. Circle the letters for your child.

❋ Read one line of the poem three times. First, just read it through. Second, read it while pointing at each word. Finally, ask your child to point as you read. Repeat with other lines if your child remains interested.

---

during circle time and introduce several early concepts of print. The home activities reinforce these concepts and give children extra practice. All these activities are quick and fun. They're designed for children to complete successfully.

Fast Start in the PreK–K Classroom

To introduce the program, explain to children that they will be working with poems and word games both at school and at home. Build their enthusiasm by emphasizing that poetry is fun to read and share. Then dive right into the first poem, reading with voice and expression. We recommend printing the poems on chart paper so that all children can see and follow along as you read. Here's a simple 5- to 10-minute routine you can use for all Fast Start activities.

1. Display the poem and read it to children two or three times. You may want to use your finger or a pointer to show the words as you read.

2. Invite children to read or recite the poem with you. Read chorally two or three times as well, again pointing to words as they are read.

3. Invite individuals or partners to recite the poem.

4. Do one or more of the school activities. Use children's interest to help you gauge how long a session should be. You can also repeat activities from one day to the next. This will not only help children learn the selected concepts, but it will also foster a feeling of success!

TIP

You may want to make classroom poetry books for children to look at during other times of the school day. If you do this, use large, bold fonts; leave room on each page for children to illustrate the poems.

Building the Home-School Connection

After the first Fast Start lesson, build on students' enthusiasm by telling them they'll get to read poems at home, too. You may want to show them how it will work, having a student role-play with you as you read a poem and do a home activity. Students may wonder whether an older sibling, grandparent, or babysitter could fill the parent's role. The answer is, "Of course!" Help children see that consistent practice is the goal. Show them the log sheet (page 18) and how to fill it out, and mention that you'll be inviting their families in to share the program with them.

Throughout the year, short, frequent classroom discussions about children's Fast Start experiences at home will also keep enthusiasm high. Remind children to return their logs sheets each week.

INTRODUCING FAST START TO FAMILIES

Although the Fast Start routine is straightforward and simple, a clear introduction for families is important. Families need to understand that they are crucial players in their children's literacy development, and it helps them to see a demonstration of the Fast Start routine. Therefore, early in the school year, we recommend offering two "Introduction to Fast Start" sessions at convenient times, such as early evening and during the day. We have found that sustained participation in the program is much higher among families who have attended introductory sessions.

Before the introductory session, make copies of the following pages for each family.

✳ "Dear Parents" letter in English and Spanish, as appropriate (pages 9–10)
✳ Log sheet (page 18)
✳ Fast Start Routine sheet in English and Spanish, as appropriate (pages 11–12)
✳ A copy of the poem and activities you will use in the demonstration

Prepare colorful pocket folders for each family, labeling each with the child's name and affixing a Fast Start Sticker. Put a set of handouts in each folder.

Then, conduct the orientation following these five easy steps:

1. Introduce the program by stressing three points:
   • This is an easy-to-do, research-based program that makes a significant difference in children's reading growth.
   • It takes only 5 to 10 minutes each night.
   • The routine has two parts: reading the poems and doing the activities.
2. Distribute the folders to families. Encourage parents and children to decorate the folders at home.
3. Do a simple demonstration so that families can see Fast Start in action. Use a volunteer to play the child's role. Demonstrate how to read to and with the child. Also show parents how to do some of the activities.
4. Review the handouts in the folder. Discuss the Log Sheet and the importance of keeping track of the work. Point out that the Fast Start Routine sheet can be used as a reference for any activity. Emphasize that the routine should be fun and simple, and parents and caregivers should take cues from children as to when they've had enough and when they want to continue.
5. Provide time for questions and encourage families to contact you if they need support sustaining Fast Start.

Dear Family,

Welcome to the new school year! Learning about reading will be an important goal for your child this year. We will work on this each day in school, but you have an important role to play at home, too! This year we will participate in the Fast Start program. Please spend 5 to 10 minutes on Fast Start activities each evening. Here is how the program works:

* Each Monday I will send two short poems, two activity pages, and a log sheet home with your child in his or her Fast Start folder.

* Each evening enjoy one of the poems together. Then spend a few minutes doing the home activities. You may want to do the same activities for two or three days in a row, especially if your child enjoys them. On the log sheet, record the amount of time you and your child spent doing Fast Start.

* Please have your child bring the log sheet and his or her Fast Start folder back to school each Monday.

Enjoy! Please contact me if you have questions or want to share information about your child. Together we will help children become strong and successful readers!

Sincerely,

Estimada familia:

¡Bienvenidos al nuevo año académico! Un objetivo importante para su hijo/a este año será que aprende sobre la lectura. Iremos trabajando en esto todos los días en la escuela, pero ¡Uds. también tienen un papel importante que desempeñar en casa! Este año vamos a participar en el programa *Fast Start*. Por favor, pasen 5 a 10 minutos todas las noches en las actividades de *Fast Start*. El programa funciona así:

✳ Todos los lunes le daré dos poemas cortos, dos páginas de actividades y una hoja de apuntes a su hijo/a para llevarlos a casa. Estarán dentro de su carpeta de *Fast Start*.

✳ Disfruten un poema juntos todas las noches. Luego, pasen unos cuantos minutos haciendo las actividades en casa. Si prefieren, pueden hacer las mismas actividades por dos o tres días seguidos, sobre todo si le gustan a su hijo/a. En la hoja de apuntes, anoten la cantidad de tiempo que Ud(s). y su hijo/a pasen en *Fast Start*.

✳ Por favor, que su hijo/a traiga la hoja de apuntes y su carpeta de *Fast Start* a la escuela todos los lunes.

¡Disfrútenlo! No duden en ponerse en contacto conmigo si tienen cualquier pregunta o si quieren compartir información sobre su hijo/a. ¡Juntos haremos que sus hijos sean lectores hábiles y exitosos!

Atentamente,

1, 2, 3, Read!
The Fast Start Routine

Fast Start combines several principles of effective reading instruction:

❋ **Read to your child.** Sit together in a comfortable, quiet, well-lit place. Read the poem aloud to your child several times. Use a natural, fluent voice. Point at the words as you read. This provides a model for your child.

❋ **Read with your child.** Invite your child to join you in reading the poem aloud. Do this several times. Don't be concerned if your child misses words. This is a supportive way to encourage reading.

❋ **Listen to your child read (or recite).** In this step, invite your child to try saying the poem by himself or herself. Your child will probably not actually be reading the poem. That's OK! This "pretend reading" is an important step towards real reading. Offer help, if necessary, and lavish praise.

❋ **Do an activity.** Keep the atmosphere game-like and relaxed. You want your child to stay engaged and to enjoy the activities. You can repeat the ones that your child seems to enjoy.

Follow this routine at least two days in a row for each poem. Record your time on the log sheet to share information with the teacher and to help you keep track of your sessions.

1, 2, 3, ¡lean!
La rutina de *Fast Start*

Fast Start utiliza varios principios para enseñar la lectura de la manera más eficaz:

* **Leer a su hijo/a.** Siéntense juntos en un lugar cómodo, tranquilo, y bien iluminado. Lea el poema a su hijo/a en voz alta varias veces. Hable con voz natural y fluida. Señale las palabras con el dedo mientras lee. Esto le da a su hijo/a un modelo para seguir.

* **Leer con su hijo/a.** Invite a su hijo/a a leer el poema con Ud. en voz alta. Hagan esto unas cuantas veces. No se preocupe si su hijo/a no lee todas las palabras. Esta es una manera amable de apoyar a su hijo/a y animarle a leer.

* **Escuche a su hijo/a mientras lee (o recita).** En este paso, anime a su hijo/a a tratar de leer el poema a solas. Es probable que su hijo/a no estará leyendo el poema de veras. ¡Está bien! Esta "lectura fingida" es un paso importante hacia la lectura verdadera. Ofrézcale su ayuda, si la necesita, y alabanzas abundantes.

* **Hagan una actividad.** Mantenga una atmósfera relajada, como si todo fuera un juego. Quiere que su hijo/a siga participando con interés y que se divierta al hacer las actividades. Pueden repetir las actividades que más le gusten a su hijo/a.

Sigan esta rutina durante por lo menos dos días seguidos por cada poema. Anote el tiempo en la hoja de apuntes para compartir esta información con el/la profesor(a) y para ayudarle a Ud. a tener un récord de estas sesiones.

MAKING FAST START WORK FOR LIMITED ENGLISH PROFICIENT FAMILIES

Families whose first language is not English can also participate in Fast Start. In order to prepare materials for them, first determine parents' or older siblings' English proficiency. The poems are very simple, so if family members can read some English, the program can proceed as with native English speakers. If family members are not proficient in English:

❋ Ask a classroom volunteer to record the poems on audiotape. Two versions of each poem will be best, one slow and deliberate and the other a fluent rendition. Children can keep these tapes in their Fast Start folders. The at-home routine can then be modified: first, parent and child look at the poem and listen to the tape several times. Then, they read together along with the taped version. Finally, the child reads (or recites) the poem by himself or herself. You may want to advise parents not to play the word games or to spend less time doing so.

❋ Family members may be learning English themselves. See how you can help both children and their families. For example, adults might practice the poems in their English classes so that they can read them at home with their children.

❋ Check with English Language Learner (ELL) teachers or tutors in your school. Because they will have knowledge about children's linguistic backgrounds, they may have more specific ideas for families. Share Fast Start information with these teachers or tutors. Children can practice the poems in their ELL classes.

Using the Activity Pages

Here are examples of the types of activities you will find on the activity pages. The activities are designed to help children learn how print works. The child does not need to read or write to do any of these activities. Adults do this work for the child. The activities are easier at the beginning of the book and more challenging later in the book. There are six activities for each poem: three for in-school use, and three for families to try at home.

You can do one activity each day at school, and parents or caregivers can do one at home. You (and parents or caregivers) can do more, if the children stay interested. The activities can be repeated from one day to the next, again if children remain interested. The activities should be game-like—have fun with them, and encourage families to do the same. Praise children when they answer correctly, and help out as needed.

Following are examples of the types of activities you will find on the activity pages. These examples are drawn from the home activities; the school activities address the same skills and follow a similar progression of challenge.

LEARNING ABOUT PRINT

Early in the book:

❋ Show your child the first word in the first line of the poem. Say, "This is the first word in this line." Then show your child the first word of the second line in the poem. Say, "This is the first word in this line." Then ask your child, "Where is the first word of this line?" [point to line 3]. Repeat with line 4.

Later in the book:

❋ Ask your child to tell you the letters that begin and end each line.

❋ Ask your child to count the words in the poem, line by line.

LEARNING ABOUT LETTERS

Early in the book:

❋ Write an uppercase and lowercase *a* on a slip of paper and show it to your child. Help your child find the *a*'s in the poem. Circle them for your child.

Later in the book:

❋ Ask your child to find:

• two words that have two letters

• three words that have three letters

• four words that have four letters

LEARNING ABOUT WORDS AND SOUNDS

Early in the book:

❋ Read the poem line by line. After you have read each line, count the words in it, and point at them. Then read the poem again, line by line. Ask your child to help you count the words in each line.

Later in the book:

❋ Say these pairs of words. Ask your child to tell you if the words start with the same sound. (You may want to exaggerate the beginning sounds.)

mother, mittens	*little, lost*	*kittens, pie*
we, you	*naughty, nice*	

Managing Fast Start: Helpful Hints

Managing the program is easy, and you'll naturally develop a management system that works for you. Here are some tips:

❋ Remind children to return log sheets, as these will help you track participation. You might suggest that families use magnets to affix the sheets to their refrigerators. To avoid being overwhelmed by paperwork, review the returned log sheets about once a month. Our research has shown that putting families in one of three categories is sufficient for program evaluation: actively involved, somewhat involved, not involved. Thus, you may want to skim returned log sheets rather than tediously summing minutes of participation.

❋ You may use the poems in any order that works for you. The word play activities are differentiated, so you can meet the needs of all children with the same poems. However, as you think about order, please note that both the poems and the accompanying activities are easier at the beginning of the book and more challenging later in the book.

❋ Most families sustain involvement in the program because they enjoy it and because they see their children benefitting. A mid-year letter (see pages 16 and 17) may encourage sustained involvement. You can also provide small incentives occasionally, such as pencils, stickers, a chance to have lunch with you, or bookmarks (see page 19) to keep interest high. Award the certificates (see page 20) at the end of the school year.

❋ If you distribute a classroom newsletter, include occasional articles about the program, perhaps with quotes from children about how much they enjoy it. You can also include reminders about the important role parents play in children's learning and answer program-related questions that have arisen.

❋ Calling a few individual families each week is another good way to encourage sustained involvement. You can use these calls to chat with families about children's literacy-related growth and to answer individual questions.

❋ Surveys and informal conversations are the easiest ways to get feedback about the program. You can send home copies of page 23, a reproducible survey for families, near the end of the school year. Analyze survey responses by noting the number of people who gave a particular response, by summarizing written comments, or by comparing responses by groups—those actively involved, those somewhat involved, and those inconsistently involved.

Dear Family,

The school year is already halfway over! Children have made lots of growth as readers this year. I know we all hope that this progress will continue. Fast Start is an important way for us to work together to support children's growth in reading. I hope you have been able to spend five minutes or so each evening with the poetry and activities. As a reminder:

* Have your child sit next to you. Read the poem to your child several times. Use your best reading voice and point to the words as you read.

* Invite your child to read along with you. Don't be concerned if your child misses words. Again, do this several times.

* Invite your child to read (or recite) the poem by himself or herself. Provide help, if needed, and praise your child's reading efforts.

* Spend a couple of minutes doing an activity.

* Record your time on the log sheet.

Most of all, enjoy!

Sincerely,

Estimada familia:

¡Ya hemos llegado a la mitad del año académico! Los niños han avanzado mucho como lectores este año. Sé que todos esperamos que este progreso continúe. *Fast Start* es una manera importante en que podemos trabajar juntos para apoyar el crecimiento de los niños como lectores. Espero que hayan podido pasar unos 5 minutos todas las noches en la poesía y otras actividades. Como recordatorio:

* Que su hijo/a se siente a su lado. Lea el poema a su hijo/a varias veces. Trate de hablar con su mejor "voz de lectura", y señale las palabras mientras lee.

* Invite a su hijo/a a que lea con Ud. No se preocupe si su hijo/a omite algunas palabras o si no las lee bien. Hagan esto unas cuantas veces.

* Pida a su hijo/a que lea (o recite) el poema a solas. Ofrézcale su ayuda, si la necesita, y sea generoso/a al elogiar los esfuerzos de su hijo/a.

* Pasen un par de minutos haciendo una actividad.

* Anoten el tiempo en la hoja de apuntes.

  Sobre todo, ¡que lo disfruten!

Atentamente,

Fast Start Log

For _____   Week of _____

Day	Poem	Time	Comments
Monday			
Tuesday			
Wednesday			
Thursday			
Friday			
Saturday			
Sunday			

SUPER STAR

Bookworm

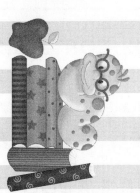

Dive Into a Great Book

This is to certify that

_____

has completed

FAST START

for Getting Ready to Read

Date _____

Signed _____

Congratulations!

Assessing Children's Progress

It's relatively easy to assess the impact that Fast Start is having on your students as readers and to gather families' opinions about the program. Here are some suggestions for both.

ASSESSING STUDENTS AS READERS

If your students already take mandated tests, you can use results to evaluate the impact of Fast Start. Simply divide the class into three groups: actively involved, somewhat involved, and inconsistently/not involved. Then record children's test scores on a chart like this:

Name	September Results	May Results	Change (+/-)

Analyzing results in this way will allow you to look at the growth of all children over the school year as well as to compare results for children with different levels of Fast Start participation.

You can informally assess children's developing awareness of print concepts as well. You may wish to do this quarterly. Here are some simple procedures:

❋ For print concepts, provide a copy of a poem or other text. Ask the child a series of questions about it, such as
  - Where does this start?
  - Where does it end?
  - Show me the first line.
  - Show me the last line.

❋ For letter knowledge, use a deck of alphabet cards (uppercase and lowercase). Make note of how many the child can recognize. An easier alternative, perhaps appropriate for 4-year-olds or at the beginning of the year, is to provide two or three cards and ask the child to find a letter that you name. For example, you might show cards for A, B, and C and ask the child, "Which one is the letter A?"

❋ For assessing knowledge about words and sounds:
  - Begin with a poem or other short text. Say to the child, "I will circle some things. You tell me if they are words." (Circle three or four things: short word, longer word, single letter

that is not a word, and multiple letters that are not words.)

- Then say to the child, "Now you take the pencil. Underline a word. Underline another word."
- Write several words from the poem or short text on separate cards. Give these to the child one at a time. Ask the child to match the card to the word in the poem or short text.
- Here are several sets of words. Say each set to the child and ask if they rhyme (sound alike):

bag	all	get	get	fire	flame
tag	ball	dog	wet	wire	flight

- Here are several sets of words. Say each set to the child and ask if they start with the same sound:

bag	tag	dog	dog	Mary	kitten
ball	ten	cat	daddy	mice	cat

✱ To evaluate children's performance on any of these tasks, decide in which category to place the child's knowledge: a) the child has mastered this concept; b) the child is developing knowledge about this concept, but has not yet mastered it; or c) this concept is beyond the child's knowledge at this time.

Be sure to share assessment results with families. And save assessment results from one year to use in family orientation for the next year. Everyone is more eager to participate if they know that their time has paid off (or will pay off).

USING SURVEYS AND INTERVIEWS

Chatting with children and surveying family members can provide additional information about Fast Start. The interview questions and surveys that follow take just a few minutes to complete. You can evaluate most responses by using three categories: yes, somewhat, no. You may also want to keep a list of suggestions for refining the program.

Children's Interview Questions

- ✱ Did you like reading the poems? Why?
- ✱ Did you like the word games? Why?
- ✱ Who read the poems and played the games with you? Do you think _____ liked this? How do you know?
- ✱ Do you think the poems and games made you a better reader? Why?
- ✱ How can I make the poems and games better for children in next year's class?

Family Survey

Dear Family,

Now that the school year is almost over, I would like your opinion of the poems and word games in the Fast Start program. Your feedback will help me refine the program for next year's class. Please use the back of the sheet for your comments. Thanks!

Sincerely,

Parent/Guardian Name_____   Child's Name_____

1. Did your child enjoy the Fast Start sessions?

   _____ yes   _____ no   _____ somewhat

2. Did you enjoy the Fast Start sessions?

   _____ yes   _____ no   _____ somewhat

3. Did your child enjoy the poems?

   _____ yes   _____ no   _____ somewhat

4. Did your child enjoy the word games?

   _____ yes   _____ no   _____ somewhat

5. Do you think Fast Start has made a difference in your child's reading?

   _____ yes   _____ no   _____ somewhat

6. What problems did you have?

7. How can I make the program better?

Encuesta para la familia

Estimada familia:

Ahora que casi se termina el año escolar, me gustaría saber su opinión sobre los poemas y juegos de palabras del programa *Fast Start*. Sus opiniones me ayudarán a pulir el programa para la clase el año que viene. Por favor, usen el envés de la hoja para escribir sus comentarios. ¡Gracias!

Atentamente,

Nombre y apellido(s) del padre/guardián _____

Nombre y apellido(s) del estudiante _____

1. ¿Le gustaron a su hijo/a las sesiones de *Fast Start*?

   _____ sí   _____ no   _____ más o menos

2. ¿A Ud. le gustaron las sesiones de Fast Start?

   _____ sí   _____ no   _____ más o menos

3. ¿A su hijo/a le gustaron los poemas?

   _____ sí   _____ no   _____ más o menos

4. ¿A su hijo/a le gustaron los juegos de palabras?

   _____ sí   _____ no   _____ más o menos

5. ¿Piensa Ud. que Fast Start ha tenido una influencia en la lectura de su hijo/a?

   _____ sí   _____ no   _____ más o menos

6. ¿Cuáles problemas experimentaron?

7. ¿Qué puedo hacer para mejorar el programa?

Play Days

How many days has
my baby to play?
Saturday, Sunday, Monday,
Tuesday, Wednesday,
Thursday, Friday,
Saturday, Sunday,
Monday.

1. Play Days

ACTIVITIES FOR SCHOOL

✳ Display the poem. Write both a lowercase and an uppercase *s* on chart paper or the board. Name the letter, then ask children to find the letter *s* in the poem by coming up and pointing to it. Circle the words for them.

✳ Display the poem. Write the word *day* on chart paper or on the board. Ask children to find the word *day* in the poem. Draw squares around the words for them.

✳ Make word cards for the days of the week, writing "Mon," "Tues," "Wednes," "Thurs," "Fri," "Satur," "Sun," and "day," each on its own card. Show children how to put two cards together to make the days of the week. Say "*Mon* plus *day* is *Monday*." Ask a child to come up and make *Monday* with the cards. Repeat with other days.

✳ ✳ ✳ ✳

ACTIVITIES FOR HOME

✳ Read the poem aloud. Then show your child the first word of the first line and say, "This is the first word in this line." Next, show your child the first word of the second line and say, "This is the first word in this line." Then point to line 3 and ask, "Where is the first word of this line?" Repeat with line 4.

✳ Read the poem aloud. Then show your child the last word of the first line and say, "This is the last word in this line." Then show your child the last word of the second line of the poem and say, "This is the last word in this line." Then point to line 3 and ask, "Where is the last word of this line?" Repeat with line 4.

✳ After reading the poem, ask your child to show you the first line. Then ask your child to show you the last line in the poem.

Ways to Play

How many ways

has my baby to play?

Trucks and toys

for girls and boys.

Dolls and balls

for them, too.

How many ways

has my baby to play?

More than just a few.

2. Ways to Play

ACTIVITIES FOR SCHOOL

* Display the poem. Write "play" on the board or chart paper. Ask children to find the word *play* in the poem. Circle this word for them.

* Play a riddle game with children. Tell them that the answers will rhyme with (sound like) *play* and that you will give them the beginning sound of the answer.
  1. This is what we do when we buy something. It starts with /p/. (*pay*)
  2. This is what we feed horses. It starts with /h/. (*hay*)
  3. This is a month in spring. It starts with /m/. (*May*)

* On a sheet of chart paper write *ay*. Tell children that this combination of letters makes the sound /ay/. Ask them to help make a list of words that have *ay* in them (such as *day*, *say*, *play*, *ray*, and *hay*). Record the words on chart paper, and practice reading them with children several times over the next few days. Have students write one or two of the words on paper or whiteboards.

✳ ✳ ✳ ✳ ✳

ACTIVITIES FOR HOME

* Read the poem aloud. Show your child the first word in the first line of the poem. Ask your child to find the first words of the other lines in the poem.

* After reading the poem aloud, write a lowercase and an uppercase *a* on a slip of paper. Show the letters to your child and name them: "This is an uppercase *A*. This is a lowercase *a*." Ask your child to find the letter *a* in the poem. Circle the letters for your child.

* Read one line of the poem three times. First, just read it through. Second, read it while pointing at each word. Finally, ask your child to point as you read. Repeat with other lines if your child remains interested.

Jack Be Nimble

Jack, be nimble,

Jack, be quick.

Jack jumps over

The candlestick.

3. Jack Be Nimble

ACTIVITIES FOR SCHOOL

✳ Do an echo reading. First, read the poem aloud. Then, reread the first line and have children repeat it after you. Continue with the rest of the lines.

✳ Read the poem aloud. Then, tell children you're going to clap the syllables, or beats, in each line. Read the poem again while clapping the syllables. Finally, invite children to clap along with you. Repeat if children's interest is sustained.

✳ Play a riddle game with children. Tell them that the answers will rhyme with (sound like) *quick*.

1. This is something you can do to a ball. You do it with your foot. (*kick*)
2. This describes you if you don't feel well. It starts with /s/. (*sick*)
3. A clock says _____ tock. (*tick*)
4. This is something we do to an ice cream cone. (*lick*)
5. This is a small branch from a tree. It starts with /st/. (*stick*)

✳ ✳ ✳ ✳ ✳

ACTIVITIES FOR HOME

✳ After reading the poem aloud, write a lowercase and an uppercase *i* on a slip of paper. Show the letters to your child and name them: "This is an uppercase *I*. This is a lowercase *i*." Ask your child to find the letter *i* in the poem. Circle the letters for your child.

✳ After reading the poem aloud, write a lowercase and an uppercase *a* on a slip of paper. Show the letters to your child and name them: "This is an uppercase *A*. This is a lowercase *a*." Ask your child to find the letter *a* in the poem. Make a square around these for your child.

✳ Read one line of the poem three times. First, just read it through. Second, read it while pointing at each word. Finally, ask your child to point as you read. Repeat with other lines if your child remains interested.

Jill Is Nimble

Jill is nimble

Jill is fast

Jill can run

And she's never last.

4. Jill Is Nimble

ACTIVITIES FOR SCHOOL

✳ Do an echo reading. First, read the poem aloud. Then, reread the first line and have children repeat it after you. Continue with the rest of the lines.

✳ Display the poem and ask children to find
- The first word in the poem
- A line that has three words
- A line that has four words
- The last word in the poem
- The letter *a* in the poem [if interest warrants, repeat with the letters *i* and *n*]

✳ Play a riddle game with the children. Tell them to find answers that will rhyme with *fast*.
1. If you break a bone you may have to wear a _____. (*cast*)
2. If you are not slow you are ____. (*fast*)
3. If something happened yesterday, it happened in the ____. (*past*)
4. The opposite of *first* is ____. (*last*)

✳ ✳ ✳ ✳ ✳

ACTIVITIES FOR HOME

✳ Read the poem aloud. It contains the common word pattern, or word family, *ast*. On a blank sheet of paper, write the words from the poem that contain this word family: *fast* and *last*. Read them to your child and, together, brainstorm other words that contain the word family. Write the words on the paper, then practice reading them with your child over the next few days.

✳ Read the poem aloud. Then tell your child you're going to clap the syllables, or beats, in each line. Read each line while clapping the syllables. Finally, invite your child to clap along.

✳ Read the poem aloud. Then read the poem again, but replace Jill's name with your child's name.

Star Light

Star light, star bright,

First star I see tonight.

I wish I may, I wish I might

Have the wish I wish tonight.

5. Star Light

ACTIVITIES FOR SCHOOL

❋ Read the poem aloud. Then tell children you're going to clap the syllables, or beats, in each line. Read the poem again while clapping the syllables. Finally, invite children to clap along with you. Repeat if children's interest is sustained.

❋ Play a riddle game with children. Tell them that the answers will rhyme with (sound like) *light*.

1. This is something we do with our teeth. It starts with /b/ (*bite*)
2. This is another word for argument. It starts with /f/. (*fight*)
3. This is how tall we are. It starts with /h/. (*height*)
4. This is a toy that flies in the sky. It is attached to a string. It starts with /k/. (*kite*)
5. This is the opposite of *day*. It starts with /n/. (*night*)

❋ Read the poem one line at a time. After you have read each line, point to the first word in the line and say, "This is the first word in the line." Then, point to the last word in the line and say, "This is the last word in the line." Read the poem again, one line at a time, and ask children to point to the first word and last word in each line.

❋ ❋ ❋ ❋ ❋

ACTIVITIES FOR HOME

❋ After reading the poem aloud, write a lowercase and an uppercase *i* on a slip of paper. Show the letters to your child and name them: "This is an uppercase *I*. This is a lowercase *i*." Then ask your child to find the letter *i* in the poem.

❋ Read the poem and point to each word as you say it. Then show your child the word *wish*. Read the poem again, pointing to each word, and stress the word *wish* each time you read it. Finally, ask your child to read with you and to point to the word *wish*.

❋ Read the poem line by line. After you have read each line, count the words in it, pointing to each word as you count it. Read the poem again, pausing at the end of each line to count the words with your child.

Second Star

Star light, star bright,

Second star I see tonight.

I wish you may,

I wish you might,

Make tomorrow out of sight!

6. Second Star

ACTIVITIES FOR SCHOOL

❋ Read the poem aloud. Then, tell children you're going to clap the syllables, or beats, in each line. Read the poem again while clapping the syllables. Finally, invite children to clap along with you. Repeat if children's interest is sustained.

❋ Write these words on the board or chart paper: *see, star, second, tonight.* Say each word while pointing to it. For each one, ask, "How many letters are in this word?" and "How many 'claps' are in this word?" Help children with these tasks as necessary.

❋ Display the poem. Then write "ight" on the board or chart paper. Ask children if they can point to the words in the poem that end in *ight* (*bright, tonight, might, sight*). Circle or write the words with *ight* on the board or chart paper.

❋ ❋ ❋ ❋ ❋

ACTIVITIES FOR HOME

❋ Do an echo reading. First, read the poem aloud. Then, reread the first line and have your child repeat it after you. Continue with the rest of the lines.

❋ After reading the poem aloud, point to each of the following words. Ask your child to tell you how many letters are in each word. Help your child count the letters as necessary.

star	wish	light	tonight

❋ Read the poem aloud. It contains the common word pattern, or word family, *ight*. On a blank sheet of paper write the words from the poem that contain this word family: *bright, tonight, might,* and *sight*. Brainstorm with your child other words that contain that word family and record the words on the paper. Practice reading the words with your child several times over the next few days.

The Old Woman Under a Hill

There was an old woman
Lived under a hill.
And if she's not gone,
She lives there still.

7. The Old Woman Under a Hill

ACTIVITIES FOR SCHOOL

* Read the poem aloud. Tell children you're going to clap the syllables, or beats, in each line. Read the poem again while clapping the syllables. Finally, invite children to clap along with you. Repeat if children's interest is sustained.

* Inform the children you are going to talk very slowly, like a turtle, and that they need to figure out what words you are saying. Then say each of these words slowly, stretching out the sounds in an exaggerated manner:

she	lives	old	there

* Write the following words from the poem on chart paper or the board: *she, old, hill, lives, if.* Point to each word and ask children, "How many letters does this word have?" Point to the letters as children count, if necessary.

＊ ＊ ＊ ＊ ＊

ACTIVITIES FOR HOME

* Read the poem line by line. After you have read each line, count the words in it, pointing to each word as you count it. Then, read the poem again, pausing at the end of each line to count the words with your child.

* Ask your child to find three words in the poem that have three letters in them.

* After reading the poem aloud, write a lowercase and an uppercase *l* on a slip of paper. Show the letters to your child and name them: "This is an uppercase *L*. This is a lowercase *l*." Ask your child to find all the words in the poem that have the letter *l* in them.

The Young Boy Is Ill

There was a young boy

Who was feeling quite ill.

He went to his doctor,

Who gave him a pill.

8. The Young Boy Is Ill

ACTIVITIES FOR SCHOOL

❋ Do an echo reading. First, read the poem aloud. Then, reread the first line and have children repeat it after you. Continue with the rest of the lines.

❋ Display the poem. Ask children to find

- the first word in the poem
- the last word in the poem
- three words that begin with *w*
- three words that have an *h* in them

❋ Play a riddle game with the children. Tell them to think of answers that rhyme with (sound like) *ill*.

1. This is a boy's name. It starts with /b/. (*Bill*)
2. This is a kind of pickle. It starts with /d/. (*dill*)
3. If you put sand in a pail, you _____ it. (*fill*)
4. This is the opposite of *won't*. It starts with /w/. (*will*)

❋ ❋ ❋ ❋ ❋

ACTIVITIES FOR HOME

❋ Do an echo reading. First, read the poem aloud. Then, reread the first line and have your child repeat it after you. Continue with the rest of the lines.

❋ After reading the poem, count the number of words in each line with your child. Then, ask your child to do this by himself or herself.

❋ Play a riddle game with your child. Ask your child to find answers that rhyme with *ill*.

1. The last word in the poem is _____. (*pill*)
2. The teacher told us to sit _____. (*still*)
3. My grandpa gave me a one-dollar _____. (*bill*)
4. If we want our glass full, we have to _____ it. (*fill*)

Little Jumping Joan

Here I am,

Little Jumping Joan.

When nobody's with me,

I'm always alone.

9. Little Jumping Joan

ACTIVITIES FOR SCHOOL

* Read the poem aloud. Then, tell children you're going to clap the syllables, or beats, in each line. Read the poem again while clapping the syllables. Finally, invite children to clap along with you. Repeat if children's interest is sustained.

* Tell children you are going to talk slowly, like a turtle, and that they need to figure out what words you are saying. Say each of these words slowly, stretching out the sounds in an exaggerated manner:

am	Joan	when	alone

* Ask children to solve the riddles with words that rhyme with (sound like) *Joan*.
  1. A dog might dig a hole in the yard to bury this. (*bone*)
  2. I am hungry for an ice cream _____. (*cone*)
  3. Do you hear that? I think the _____ is ringing. (*phone*)
  4. This is something the sun did yesterday. It starts with /sh/. (*shone*)
  5. When I am by myself, I am all _____. (*alone*)

* * * * *

ACTIVITIES FOR HOME

* After reading the poem aloud, write a lowercase and uppercase *i* on a slip of paper. Show the letters to your child and name them: "This is an uppercase *I*. This is a lowercase *i*." Ask your child to find words in the poem that contain the letter *i*.

* Read the poem aloud. Then, show your child these words in the poem and ask him or her to count the letters in each.

here	am	with	alone

* After reading the poem, ask your child to find:
  • the first word in the poem
  • the first line in the poem
  • the last word in the poem
  • the last line in the poem

Little Jumping Jim

Here I am,

Little Jumping Jim.

When Tim is with me,

I always jump with him.

10. Little Jumping Jim

ACTIVITIES FOR SCHOOL

❋ Read the poem aloud. Tell children you're going to clap the syllables, or beats, in each line. Read the poem again while clapping the syllables. Finally, invite children to clap along with you. Repeat if children's interest is sustained.

❋ Tell children you are going to talk like a turtle and that they need to figure out what words you are saying. Say each of these words slowly, stretching out the sounds in an exaggerated manner:

little	jumping	Jim	always	when

❋ Play a riddle game with the children. Have the children find answers that rhyme with (sound like) *jump*.

1. I hit my head and now I have a _____. (*bump*)
2. The _____ truck carries big loads of dirt. (*dump*)
3. To fill my basketball, I have to _____ air into it. (*pump*)
4. Mom stirred the batter until there wasn't a single _____ (*lump*).

❋ ❋ ❋ ❋ ❋

ACTIVITIES FOR HOME

❋ Read the poem aloud. First, move your finger under the first line of the poem and ask your child to point to the first word in the line. Next, ask your child to point to the last word in the line. Repeat with the other lines.

❋ Read the poem aloud. Then, do an exaggerated reading: Read the words slowly and deliberately, allowing your child to hear all the sounds in each word.

❋ Read the poem aloud and ask your child:

1. What sound do you hear at the end of all these words: *me*, *tee*, *fee*, and *key*?
2. What sound do you hear at the beginning of these words: *jumping* and *Jim*?
3. What sound do you hear at the end of these words: *Jim*, *Tim*, and *him*?

To Market

To market, to market

To buy a fat pig.

Home again, home again

Jiggety-jig.

11. To Market

ACTIVITIES FOR SCHOOL

❋ Tell children you are going to talk like a turtle and that they need to figure out what words you are saying. Then, say each of these words slowly, stretching out the sounds in an exaggerated manner:

home	again	fat	market

❋ Read the poem aloud. Then tell children you're going to clap the syllables, or beats, in each line. Read the poem again while clapping the syllables. Finally, invite children to clap along with you. Afterwards, draw children's attention to short words (*to, buy, fat, pig*—one clap each) and long words (*market*—2 claps, *jiggety-jig*—4 claps).

❋ Write the following words from the poem on chart paper or the board. For each word, ask, "How many letters does this word have?" Point to the letters as children count, if necessary:

to	fat	pig	home	a

* * * * *

ACTIVITIES FOR HOME

❋ Read one line of the poem three times. First, just read it through. Next, read it while pointing at each word. Finally, ask your child to point as you read. Repeat with other lines if your child remains interested.

❋ Read the poem line by line. After you have read each line, count the words in it, pointing to each word as you count it. Then, read the poem again, pausing at the end of each line to count the words with your child.

❋ After reading the poem, ask your child to find one word with two letters. Then, ask your child to find three words with three letters. Finally, ask your child to find one word with four letters. (Your child does not need to say the words. He or she only needs to point to them.)

A Fat Hen

To market, to market
I'll buy a fat hen.
Then home again,
home again
Jiggety-jen.

12. A Fat Hen

ACTIVITIES FOR SCHOOL

✳ Read the poem aloud. Then, tell children you're going to clap the syllables in each line. Read the poem again while clapping the syllables. Finally, invite children to clap along with you. Repeat if children's interest is sustained.

✳ Tell children you are going to talk like a turtle and that they need to figure out what words you are saying. Say each of these words slowly, stretching out the sounds in an exaggerated manner:

jiggety	jen	again	hen

✳ Ask students:
  1. What sound do you hear at the beginning of these words? *jiggety, Jen*
  2. What sound do you hear in the middle of these words? *again, jiggety*
  3. What sound do you hear at the end of these words? *again, hen, Jen*

＊ ＊ ＊ ＊ ＊

ACTIVITIES FOR HOME

✳ Read the poem aloud. Then do an exaggerated reading: Read the words slowly and deliberately, allowing your child to hear all the sounds in each word.

✳ After reading the poem, say each of these words. Ask your child, "Does this word start with the sound /m/?"

market	dog	milk	juice	apple	mud

✳ Read the poem aloud. After you have read the first line, count the words in it, pointing to each word as you count it. Then, ask your child to count the words in the line, helping out if needed. Repeat for the rest of the lines.

Rock-a-Bye Baby

Rock-a-bye baby

on the tree top.

When the wind blows,

the cradle will rock.

When the bough breaks,

the cradle will fall.

And down will come baby,

cradle and all.

13. Rock-a-Bye Baby

ACTIVITIES FOR SCHOOL

✳ Read the poem aloud. Then, tell children you're going to clap the syllables in each line. Read the poem again while clapping the syllables. Finally, invite children to clap along with you. Repeat if children's interest is sustained.

✳ Write the following words from the poem on chart paper or the board. For each word, ask, "How many letters does this word have?" If necessary, point to the letters as children count.

and	rock	all	baby	tree

✳ Challenge children to solve these riddles. Tell them that all answers are words in the poem.
1. I am the opposite of *bottom*. I start with /t/. (*top*)
2. I mean to move back and forth slowly. I start with /r/. (*rock*)
3. I am a newborn person. I start with /b/. (*baby*)
4. I am what the wind does. I start with /bl/. (*blows*)

✳ ✳ ✳ ✳ ✳

ACTIVITIES FOR HOME

✳ Read the poem aloud. Then, show your child these words in the poem and ask your child to count the letters in each:

rock	baby	wind	fall	and

✳ After reading the poem, ask your child to find:
• The first line in the poem
• The last line in the poem
• The letter *a* in two words
• The letter *b* in two words

✳ After reading the poem, ask your child to find:
• the first word in the poem
• the last word in the poem
• a word that has three letters
• a word that has four letters

Daddy Will Catch Them

Rock-a-bye baby
on the tree top.
When the wind blows,
the cradle will rock.
When the bough breaks,
the cradle may fall.
But Daddy
will catch them,
cradle and all.

14. Daddy Will Catch Them

ACTIVITIES FOR SCHOOL

❋ After reading the poem, ask children:

1. What sound does the *c* in *cradle* make? How many claps does *cradle* have?

2. What sound does the *d* in *Daddy* make? How many claps does *Daddy* have?

3. What sound does the *b* in *baby* make? How many claps does *baby* have?

❋ Display the poem. Ask children:

• What is the first letter in the first line? What is the last letter in the first line?

• What is the first letter in the second line? What is the last letter in the second line?

• What is the first letter in the third line? What is the last letter in the third line?

• What is the first letter in the fourth line? What is the last letter in the fourth line?

❋ Play a riddle game with children. Tell them to find answers that rhyme with *top*.

1. The opposite of *go* is _____. (*stop*)

2. To clean the floor you must use a _____ .(*mop*)

3. Another word for a policeman is a ___. (*cop*)

4. When you go to the mall you _____. (*shop*)

* * * * *

ACTIVITIES FOR HOME

❋ After reading the poem aloud, write a lowercase *c* on a slip of paper. Show it to your child and say, "This is lowercase *c*." Have your child point to words that begin with the letter *c*. Now, write a lowercase and an uppercase *b* on a slip of paper. Show the letters to your child and name them. Have your child point to words that begin with the letter *b*.

❋ Read the poem aloud. It contains the common word pattern, or word family, *all*. On a blank sheet of paper, write the words from the poem that contain this word family: *fall* and *all*. Read them to your child and, together, brainstorm other words that contain the word family. Write the words on the paper and practice reading them with your child over the next few days.

❋ Read the poem. Read it again, but this time replace the word *Daddy* with your child's name.

Five Toes

This little piggy went to market.

This little piggy stayed home.

This little piggy had roast beef.

This little piggy had none.

And this little piggy cried,

"Wee, wee, wee!"

all the way home.

15. Five Toes

ACTIVITIES FOR SCHOOL

✳ Display the poem. Show children the word *this*. Ask them to find the word in the poem and count how many times they see it (four). Repeat with *little* and *piggy*.

✳ Ask children to solve the riddles with words that rhyme with (sound like) *had*.

1. The opposite of *good* is ____. (*bad*)
2. Another word for *father* is ____. (*dad*)
3. Another word for *angry*; it starts with /m/. (*mad*)
4. A computer mouse sits on a mouse _____. (*pad*)
5. When we frown, we are feeling ____. (*sad* or *mad*)

✳ Tell children you are going to talk slowly, like a turtle, and that they need to figure out what words you are saying. Then, say each of these words slowly, stretching out the sounds in an exaggerated manner:

little	home	this	went	market

* * * *

ACTIVITIES FOR HOME

✳ Read one line of the poem three times. First, just read it through. Next, read it while pointing to each word. Finally, ask your child to point as you read. Repeat with other lines if your child remains interested.

✳ Read the poem line by line. After you have read each line, count the words in it, pointing to each word as you count it. Then, read the poem again, pausing at the end of each line to count the words with your child.

✳ After reading the poem, ask your child to find five words that have four letters in them.

More Little Piggies

This little piggy went to France.

This little piggy stayed here.

This little piggy learned to dance,

While this little piggy would cheer.

And this little piggy cried

And cried some big fat tears.

16. More Little Piggies

ACTIVITIES FOR SCHOOL

❋ Display the poem and read it aloud. Then, ask children to find words in the poem that rhyme with:

France	here

❋ Display the poem. Ask children to find the letter *g* in the poem. Circle the letters as children point to them. Repeat for the letter *t*.

❋ Ask children:

- What sound do you hear in the middle of the word *piggy*?
- What sound do you hear in the middle of the word *little*?

❋ ❋ ❋ ❋ ❋

ACTIVITIES FOR HOME

❋ After reading the poem, ask your child to find the letter *c* in it. Circle the letters for your child as he or she points to them.

❋ After reading the poem, ask your child to find the letter *l* in it. Circle the letters for your child as he or she points to them.

❋ Write the following sets of words on a sheet of paper:

cheer, dance, cried	little, learned, here

Show the first set to your child and ask, "Which word does not begin with *c*?" Then, show the second set of words and ask, "Which word does not begin with *l*?"

Diddle Diddle Dumpling

Diddle diddle dumpling,

my son John.

Went to bed

with his stockings on.

One shoe off,

and one shoe on.

Diddle diddle dumpling,

my son John.

17. Diddle Diddle Dumpling

ACTIVITIES FOR SCHOOL

❋ Tell children you are going to talk like a turtle and that they need to figure out what words you are saying. Then, say each of these words slowly, stretching out the sounds in an exaggerated manner:

son	shoe	John	my

❋ Ask children to solve the riddles with words that rhyme with (sound like) *bed*:

1. a color (*red*)
2. a boy's name that starts with /t/ (*Ted*)
3. what we sew with; needle and _____ (*thread*)
4. not alive (*dead*)
5. rip into tiny pieces; starts with /shr/ (*shred*)

❋ Display the poem. Ask children to find two lines that have the same number of words and tell how many words are in each of those lines. Then, ask children to find two lines that are exactly the same.

* * * * *

ACTIVITIES FOR HOME

❋ After reading the poem aloud, write a lowercase and an uppercase *d* on a slip of paper. Show the letters to your child and name them. Ask your child to find words with the letter *d* from the poem.

❋ After reading the poem aloud, point to the lines in the poem, one by one. Ask your child to count the number of words in each line.

❋ After reading the poem, show your child the word *son*. Ask your child to find it in the poem. Repeat with *my* and *John*.

My Girl Mag

Diddle diddle dumpling,

my girl Mag.

Loved to play

with her dog named Tag.

He chewed on a bone,

and he chewed on a rag.

Diddle diddle dumpling,

my girl Mag.

18. My Girl Mag

ACTIVITIES FOR SCHOOL

✳ Display the poem. Write an uppercase and a lowercase *d* on chart paper or the board. Ask children to come up and circle all the words that begin with *d*.

✳ Display the poem. Point out that the line *Diddle diddle dumpling* is repeated in the poem. Have children come up and point to the lines. Then ask them if there are any other lines that are repeated in the poem.

✳ Play a riddle game with the children. Have the children find answers that rhyme with *play*.

1. The month before June is _____. (*May*)
2. Another word for *yes* is _____. (*okay*)
3. Horses eat _____. (*hay*)
4. We go sailing in the _____. (*bay*)
5. To speak is to _____. (*say*)

✳ ✳ ✳ ✳

ACTIVITIES FOR HOME

✳ Read the poem aloud. Then, tell your child you're going to clap the syllables, or beats, in each line. Read each line while clapping the syllables. Finally, invite your child to clap along.

✳ Read the poem aloud. It contains the common word pattern, or word family, *ag*. On a blank sheet of paper, write the words from the poem that contain this word family: *Mag*, *Tag*, and *rag*. Read them to your child and, together, brainstorm other words that contain the word family. Write the words on the paper and practice reading them with your child over the next few days.

✳ After reading the poem aloud, ask your child, "What sound do you hear at the beginning of *my* and *Mag*?" Next ask, "What sound do you hear at the end of *Mag* and *Tag*?"

Jack Sprat

Jack Sprat could eat no fat;

His wife could eat no lean.

So between them both,

They cleared the cloth

And licked the platter clean.

19. Jack Sprat

ACTIVITIES FOR SCHOOL

✳ Read the poem aloud. Tell children you're going to clap the syllables in each line. Read the poem again while clapping the syllables. Finally, invite children to clap along with you. Repeat if children's interest is sustained.

✳ Tell children you are going to talk like a turtle and that they need to figure out what words you are saying. Then, say each of these words slowly, stretching out the sounds in an exaggerated manner:

| fat | lean | wife | licked | clean |

✳ Play a riddle game with children. Tell them that the answers will rhyme with (sound like) *fat*.

1. We hit a baseball with a _____. (*bat*)
2. This small animal says "meow." (*cat*)
3. The opposite of *skinny* is _____. (*fat*)
4. On the top of your head, you could wear a _____. (*hat*)
5. This is a boy's name. It starts with /m/. (*Matt*)
6. This is a soft touch or tap. It starts with /p/. (*pat*)

✳ ✳ ✳ ✳ ✳

ACTIVITIES FOR HOME

✳ Read one line of the poem three times. First, just read it through. Next, read it while pointing to each word. Finally, ask your child to point as you read. Repeat with other lines if your child remains interested.

✳ Read the poem line by line. After you have read each line, count the words in it, pointing to each word as you count it. Then, read the poem again, pausing at the end of each line to count the words with your child.

✳ After reading the poem, ask your child to find four words with three letters in them.

Spoon, Fork, and Knife

Jack Sprat could eat no fat;

His wife could eat no lean.

So between man and wife,

With spoon, fork, and knife,

They licked the platter clean.

20. Spoon, Fork, and Knife

ACTIVITIES FOR SCHOOL

✲ Display the poem. Ask children to identify the words in the poem that contain the letter *a*. Underline these words as children point them out.

✲ This poem contains the common word pattern, or word family, *at*. On chart paper or the board, write the words from the poem that contain this word family: *Sprat* and *fat*. Brainstorm with children other words that contain that word family. Record the words and practice reading them with children several times over the next few days.

✲ Play a riddle game with the children. Have the children find answers that will rhyme with *fat*.

1. The dog chased the _____. (*cat*)

2. I don't want this. I want some of _____. (*that*)

3. A piece of paper is _____. (*flat*)

4. Before you go into the house, wipe your feet on the ___. (*mat*).

5. The girl will gently ___ the dog's head. (*pat*)

✳ ✳ ✳ ✳ ✳

ACTIVITIES FOR HOME

✲ Do an echo reading. First, read the poem aloud. Then, reread the first line and have your child repeat it after you. Continue with the rest of the lines.

✲ Read the poem aloud. It contains the common word pattern, or word family, *ean*. On a blank sheet of paper, write the words from the poem that contain this word family: *lean* and *clean*. Read them to your child and, together, brainstorm other words that contain the word family. Write the words on the paper and practice reading them with your child over the next few days.

✲ Ask your child to solve these riddles. Answers will rhyme with *lean*. (Note: if these words are on your brainstormed list, show them to your child after he or she solves the riddles.)

1. I describe someone who is not very nice. I start with the sound /m/. (*mean*)

2. I am a vegetable. I am green. I start with the sound /b/. (*bean*)

3. I am the opposite of *dirty*. I start with the sound /cl/. (*clean*)

Hey Diddle Diddle

Hey diddle diddle,

The cat and the fiddle,

The cow jumped over

The moon.

The little dog laughed

To see such a sport,

And the dish ran away

With the spoon.

21. Hey Diddle Diddle

ACTIVITIES FOR SCHOOL

✳ Display the poem. Ask children to find:
- two words that have two *d*'s
- two words that have two *o*'s
- four words that have three letters

✳ Make a two-column chart labeled "Living Thing" and "Not a Living Thing." Ask children to help you decide where these words from the poem go on the chart:

cat	fiddle	cow	moon	dog	spoon

✳ Do a word-ladder activity:
1. Which animal in the poem has a fiddle? (*cat*)
2. Change the first sound of *cat* to make a new word. This is something we wear on our heads. (*hat*)
3. Change the middle sound of *hat* to make a new word. This is the opposite of *cold*. (*hot*)
4. Change the ending sound of *hot* to make another word for *pig*. (*hog*)
5. What word rhymes with *hog* and tells which animal laughs in the poem? (*dog*)

✳ ✳ ✳ ✳ ✳

ACTIVITIES FOR HOME

✳ After reading the poem aloud, write a lowercase *d* on a slip of paper. Show it to your child and name it. Then, ask your child to find words in the poem that contain *d*.

✳ After reading the poem, ask your child to find:
- a line that begins and ends with the letter *t*
- two lines that have three words
- the longest line in the poem. How many words does it have? (six)

✳ After reading the poem, ask your child to find the word *the* in the poem. *The* appears seven times. See if your child can find them all. Circle the words as your child finds them and help your child count the words he or she has found.

The Sleeping Dog

Hey diddle diddle,

The cat and the fiddle,

The cow jumped onto the hay.

The little dog laughed

To see such a sport,

And slept for the rest

Of the day.

22. The Sleeping Dog

ACTIVITIES FOR SCHOOL

✳ This poem contains the common word pattern, or word family, *ow*. Write *cow* on chart paper or the board and ask children to brainstorm other words that contain that word family. Record their words and practice reading them with children over the next few days.

✳ Ask children to solve these riddles with words that rhyme with (sound like) *cow*:

1. At the end of the show, the actors took a _____. (*bow*)

2. I am impatient; I want it right ___! (*now*)

3. I can begin a question. I start with /h/. (*how*)

✳ Ask children:

• What sound do you hear at the beginning of *cat* and *cow*?

• What sound do you hear at the end of *cat* and *sport*?

✳ ✳ ✳ ✳ ✳

ACTIVITIES FOR HOME

✳ Read the poem aloud. Then, ask your child to find:

• two words that start with the letter *d*

• two words that end with the letter *d*

• two words that start with the letter *t*

• two words that end with the letter *t*

✳ Read the poem aloud. It contains the common word pattern, or word family, *ay*. On a blank sheet of paper, write the words from the poem that contain this word family: *hay* and *day*. Read them to your child and, together, brainstorm other words that contain the word family. Write the words on the paper and practice reading them with your child over the next few days.

✳ Ask your child to solve these riddles. Answers contain the word family *ay*. If these words are on the chart you and your child created above, point them out after your child answers the riddles.

1. I am what you like to do after school. I start with the sound /pl/. (*play*)

2. A new one of me starts each morning. I start with the sound /d/. (*day*)

3. I am what horses eat. I start with the sound /h/. (*hay*)

4. I am a kind of bird. Sometimes I am blue. I start with the sound /j/. (*jay*)

Bye Baby Bunting

Bye, baby bunting

Daddy's gone a-hunting

To get a little rabbit skin

To wrap his baby bunting in.

23. Bye Baby Bunting

ACTIVITIES FOR SCHOOL

❋ Display the poem and read it aloud. Point to each line in the poem and ask children to count how many words are in it.

❋ Make a three-column chart labeled "Beginning," "Middle," "Both." Display the poem and point to these words from the poem. For each word, ask where the letter *b* is located and put the word in the appropriate column on the chart.

| bye | baby | bunting | rabbit |

❋ Play a riddle game with children. Tell them that the answers will rhyme with (sound like) *skin*.

1. Fish have this. It starts with /f/. (*fin*)
2. Cans are made of _____. (*tin*)
3. The opposite of *lose* is _____. (*win*)
4. The opposite of *fat* is _____. (*thin*)
5. This is a racket, a lot of noise. This word starts with /d/. (*din*)

❋ ❋ ❋ ❋ ❋

ACTIVITIES FOR HOME

❋ After reading the poem, ask your child to find
  • two words with one *b*
  • two words with two *b*'s
  • the line in which all words begin with *b*

❋ After reading the poem, have your child find words in the poem that contain the letter *i*.

❋ Ask your child, "How many lines have three words?" (two) "How many lines have six words?" (two)

Baby Bopping

Bye bye, baby Bopping

Mommy's gone a-shopping

To buy a brand new soft bed

To lay down baby Bopping's

Dear little head.

24. Baby Bopping

ACTIVITIES FOR SCHOOL

✳ Do an exaggerated reading of the poem. Say the words slowly and deliberately, allowing children to hear all the sounds in each word.

✳ Display the poem. Then, read it while you clap the syllables. Read it again, inviting children to read and clap with you.

✳ Display the poem and ask children to point to the *b*'s in the poem. Ask what sound they hear at the beginning of the words: *bye*, *baby*, *bopping*, *buy*, and *brand*.

✳ ✳ ✳ ✳ ✳

ACTIVITIES FOR HOME

✳ Read the poem line by line. At the end of each line, have your child find words that begin with the letter *b*. Then ask, "How many *b* words are there in this line?"

✳ Read the poem aloud. Tell your child you're going to clap the syllables, or beats, in each line. Read each line while clapping the syllables. Finally, invite your child to clap along.

✳ Ask your child to solve these riddles with words that rhyme with (sound like) *shop*.
  1. I am what bunnies do to move. I start with the sound /h/. (*hop*)
  2. I am something you use to clean the floor. I start with the sound /m/. (*mop*)
  3. I am the opposite of *go*. I start with the sound /st/. (*stop*)
  4. I am the opposite of *bottom*. I start with the sound /t/. (*top*)

For Baby

You shall have an apple,

You shall have a plum,

You shall have a rattle,

When papa comes home.

25. For Baby

ACTIVITIES FOR SCHOOL

❋ Make a three-column chart labeled "Beginning," "Middle," "End." Display the poem and show children these words. For each, ask where the letter *a* is located, and put the word in the appropriate column on the chart,

shall	apple	rattle	papa	an

❋ Display the poem. Ask children to find all the words that contain four letters. Circle them.

❋ Display the poem. Ask children, "Where is the first line? How many words does it have?" Repeat for the remaining lines.

❋ ❋ ❋ ❋ ❋

ACTIVITIES FOR HOME

❋ Read one line of the poem three times. First, just read it through. Next, read it while pointing to each word. Finally, ask your child to point as you read. Repeat with other lines if your child remains interested.

❋ Read the poem line by line. After you have read each line, count the words in it, pointing to each word as you count it. Then, read the poem again, pausing at the end of each line to count the words with your child.

❋ After reading the poem, write the word *you* on a slip of paper. Ask your child to find this word in the poem. Repeat with the words *shall* and *have*.

Apples and Pears

You may have an apple,

You may have a pear,

You may have a rattle,

When papa gets here.

26. Apples and Pears

ACTIVITIES FOR SCHOOL

✳ Do an echo reading. First, read the poem aloud. Then, reread the first line and have children repeat it after you. Continue with the rest of the lines.

✳ Display the poem and count the words in each line. Ask children, "Which lines have five words? Which line has only four words?"

✳ Play a riddle game with children. Tell them to find answers that rhyme with (sound like) *pear*.

1. The baby held her teddy ____. (*bear*)
2. I do not _____ for scary movies. (*care*)
3. The page ripped, so it had a ____. (*tear*)

✳ ✳ ✳ ✳ ✳

ACTIVITIES FOR HOME

✳ Read the poem once through. Then, read it again, but replace *you* with your child's name.

✳ Read the poem aloud. It contains the common word pattern, or word family, *et*. On a blank sheet of paper, write the word from the poem that contains this word family: *get*. Read it to your child and, together, brainstorm other words that contain the word family. Write the words on the paper and practice reading them with your child over the next few days.

✳ Ask your child to solve these riddles. Answers will rhyme with (sound like) *get*. If the answers are on the chart you and your child made, point the words out after your child has solved the riddles.

1. I am the opposite of *dry*. I start with the sound /w/. (*wet*)
2. I am an airplane. I start with the sound /j/. (*jet*)
3. I am an animal that lives in the house. I can be a dog or a cat. I start with the sound /p/. (*pet*)

One, Two, Buckle My Shoe

One, two
Buckle my shoe.
Three, four
Knock at the door.
Five, six
Pick up sticks.
Seven, eight
Lay them straight.
Nine, ten
A good, fat hen.

27. One, Two, Buckle My Shoe

ACTIVITIES FOR SCHOOL

✳ Display the poem. Ask children to find the number words (*one*, *two*, etc.). Circle each word for them.

✳ Make ten sets of cards for number-word–numeral pairs for the numbers one through ten. For example, one set would have one card with the word *one* written on it; the other card would have the number *1* written on it. Display the pairs for *one* through *five* on a pocket chart or with magnets. Invite children to match the word and the number. Repeat for numbers *six* through *ten*.

✳ Shuffle the numeral cards. Ask children to help you put them back in order.

✳ ✳ ✳ ✳ ✳

ACTIVITIES FOR HOME

✳ Read the poem. Reread it, pausing at the end of lines 2, 4, 6, 8, and 10. Ask your child to provide the missing words. For example, say "One, two, buckle my _____." Your child should answer "shoe."

✳ After reading the poem, ask your child to find the lines that have two words. Ask your child to find the lines that have three words.

✳ After reading the poem, ask your child to find:
   • a word that starts with *o*
   • a word with *o* in the middle
   • a word that starts with *t*
   • a word that ends with *t*

Meet Mary Sue

One, two

Meet Mary Sue.

Three, four

Open the door.

Five, six

See baby chicks.

Seven, eight

Don't they look great?

Nine, ten

Let's do it again.

28. Meet Mary Sue

ACTIVITIES FOR SCHOOL

❋ Do an echo reading. First, read the poem aloud. Then, reread the first line and have children repeat it after you. Continue with the rest of the lines.

❋ Display the poem. Ask children to identify which lines have two words in them. Count the number of two-word lines.

❋ The poem contains the common word pattern, or word family, *en*. On chart paper or the board, write the word from the poem that contains this word family (*ten*) and ask children to brainstorm other words that contain the word family. Record the words and practice reading them with children over the next few days.

* * * * *

ACTIVITIES FOR HOME

❋ Read the poem one time through. Replace *Mary Sue* with your child's name.

❋ Read the poem aloud. It contains the common word pattern, or word family, *ook*. On a blank sheet of paper, write the word from the poem that contains this word family (*look*) and brainstorm other words that contain the word family. Write the words on the paper and practice reading them with your child over the next few days.

❋ Ask your child to solve these riddles. Answers will rhyme with (sound like) *look*. If answers are on the chart you made, show them to your child after he or she solves the riddles.

1. I am what you do in the kitchen. I start with the sound /k/. (*cook*)
2. I am something to read. I start with the sound /b/. (*book*)
3. I am shaped like the letter J. You use me to catch fish or to hang up your coat. I start with the sound /h/. (*hook*)

The Little Girl With a Curl

There was a little girl
who had a little curl
right in the middle of
her forehead.
When she was good,
she was very, very good,
and when she was bad,
she was horrid.

29. The Little Girl With a Curl

ACTIVITIES FOR SCHOOL

❋ Read the poem aloud. Then, tell children you're going to clap the syllables in each line. Read the poem again while clapping the syllables. Finally, invite children to clap along with you. Repeat if children's interest is sustained.

❋ Make a three-column chart labeled "Beginning," "Middle," "End." Point to each of the following words in the poem and ask where the *t*'s are located. Put the words in the appropriate columns on the chart:

there	little	right	the

❋ Play a riddle game with children. Ask them to find answers that rhyme with (sound like) *bad*.
1. This is another name for *father*. (*dad*)
2. Mary _____ a little lamb. (*had*)
3. This is an old-fashioned word for *boy*. It starts with /l/. (*lad*)
4. This is another word for *angry*. (*mad*)
5. This is the opposite of *happy*. (*sad*)

❋ ❋ ❋ ❋ ❋

ACTIVITIES FOR HOME

❋ After reading the poem, ask your child to find words that have the same letter two times, right together. (*little, middle, good, horrid*)

❋ Read the poem and show your child the word *little*. Ask him or her to find two lines in the poem that have the word *little* in them. Repeat with *good* and *she*.

❋ Read the poem line by line. After you have read each line, count the words in it, pointing to each word as you count it. Then, read the poem again, pausing at the end of each line to count the words with your child.

The Curl on Top of Her Head

There is a girl
Who has a curl
Right on top of her head.
She loves to go outside
And ride on her sled.
In the summertime,
She likes to read in bed.

30. The Curl on Top of Her Head

ACTIVITIES FOR SCHOOL

❋ Display the poem and read it aloud. Then, read it again, line by line. For each line, ask children:

- How many words are in the line?
- What is the first letter in the line?
- What is the last letter in the line?

❋ Do an echo reading. Read the poem aloud, then reread the first line and have children repeat it after you. Continue with the rest of the lines.

❋ Ask children:

Do these words start with the same sound?

       girl, good   right, ride   top, curl

Do these words end with the same sound?

       head, sled   right, ride   girl, curl

❋ ❋ ❋ ❋ ❋

ACTIVITIES FOR HOME

❋ Do an echo reading. Read the poem aloud, then reread the first line and have your child repeat it after you. Continue with the rest of the lines.

❋ Read the poem aloud. It contains the common word pattern, or word family, *op*. On a blank sheet of paper, write the word from the poem that contains this word family (*top*), and brainstorm other words that contain the word family. Write the words on the paper and practice reading them with your child over the next few days.

❋ Ask your child to solve these riddles. Answers will rhyme with (sound like) *top*. If the answer appears on the chart you made with your child, point it out. If not, add the word to the chart.

1. I am the opposite of *go*. I start with the sound /st/. (*stop*)
2. I mean "to cut into little pieces." I start with the sound /ch/. (*chop*)
3. You can do this at a store. I start with the sound /sh/. (*shop*)
4. If you jump up and down on one foot, you _____. (*hop*)
5. I can clean a floor. I start with the sound /m/. (*mop*)

The Boy in the Barn

A little boy went into a barn,

And lay down on some hay.

An owl came out and flew about,

And the little boy ran away.

31. The Boy in the Barn

ACTIVITIES FOR SCHOOL

✳ Read the poem aloud. Then tell children you're going to clap the syllables in each line. Read the poem again while clapping the syllables. Finally, invite children to clap along with you. Repeat if children's interest is sustained.

✳ Display the poem and ask children to count the words in each line. Next, return to lines 2 and 3. Have children count the words and then, with your help, clap the syllables. Help them see that some words are short (one clap) and others are longer (two claps).

✳ Display the poem and ask children:

• What letter begins each line in the poem?

• What two lines end in the same letter?

• What two lines have the word *little*? (Show children the word; don't expect them to recognize it by sight.)

• What three lines have the word *and*? (Again, show children the word.)

• What two lines have the word *boy*? (Show children the word.)

✳ ✳ ✳ ✳ ✳

ACTIVITIES FOR HOME

✳ Read one line of the poem three times. First, just read it through. Next, read it while pointing at each word. Finally, ask your child to point as you read. Repeat with other lines if your child remains interested.

✳ Read the poem line by line. After you have read each line, count the words in it, pointing to each word as you count it. When you have finished, invite your child to read each line with you, and then to count the words in each line.

✳ After reading the poem, ask your child to find the *a*'s in the poem.

Boy in the Shop

A little boy went into a shop,

To buy a brand new toy.

His mother gave him

The money to pay.

And the boy was filled with joy.

32. Boy in the Shop

ACTIVITIES FOR SCHOOL

❋ Ask children to solve the riddles with words that rhyme with (sound like) *pop*.

1. I am what the little boy went into. I start with /sh/. (*shop*)
2. I am the opposite of *go*. I start with /st/. (*stop*)
3. I am the opposite of *bottom*. I start with /t/. (*top*)
4. I mean "to cut something into small pieces." I start with /ch/. (*chop*)

❋ Display the poem and circle the words listed below. Then, make a two-column chart labeled "One Syllable" and "Two Syllables." Say each word and ask children to help you decide where it goes on the chart.

> little   boy   brand   mother   money   filled

❋ Display the poem and ask children to find:

- two words that begin with *m*
- three words that begin with *b*
- a word with two *t*'s in the middle
- a word with two *l*'s in the middle

＊ ＊ ＊ ＊ ＊

ACTIVITIES FOR HOME

❋ Read the poem. Then, read it again, line by line. After you have read each line, invite your child to read it with you, and then to count the number of words in the line.

❋ Read the poem aloud. It contains the common word pattern, or word family, *oy*. On a blank sheet of paper, write the words from the poem that contain this word family: *joy*, *boy*, and *toy*. Read them to your child and, together, brainstorm other words that contain the word family. Write the words on the paper and practice reading them with your child over the next few days.

❋ After reading the poem, ask your child:

Do these words start with the same sound?

boy, buy   mother, money   pay, shop

Do these words end with the same sound?

boy, toy   pay, shop   and, brand

Pease Porridge

Pease porridge hot,

Pease porridge cold,

Pease porridge in the pot

Nine days old.

Some like it hot,

Some like it cold,

Some like it in the pot

Nine days old.

33. Pease Porridge

ACTIVITIES FOR SCHOOL

✳ Make word cards for *hot, cold,* and *old*. Display the poem and read it aloud. Then, shuffle the cards and give one to a child. The child should find that word in the poem. Shuffle the cards again, give another card to another child, and have that child find it in the poem, and so forth.

✳ Display the poem and help children "voice-point" the lines by

  • reading each line two times, pointing at each word as you read, and

  • inviting children to read and point along with you.

✳ Make a two-column chart labeled "Beginning" and "Middle." Display the poem and show children the following words. For each, ask where the letter *i* is, then put the word in the appropriate column on the chart:

porridge	like	in	it	nine

✳ ✳ ✳ ✳ ✳

ACTIVITIES FOR HOME

✳ Read one line of the poem three times. First, just read it through. Next, read it while pointing to each word. Finally, ask your child to point as you read. Repeat with other lines if your child remains interested.

✳ Read each line of the poem. Then, count the words in the line. When you have finished, invite your child to read each line with you, and then to count the words in each line.

✳ After reading the poem, write the word *some* on a slip of paper and show it to your child. Ask your child to find this word in the poem. Repeat with *like, hot,* and *cold*.

Pease Porridge Cold

Pease porridge cold,

Pease porridge hot,

Pease porridge

Nine days old

Sitting in the pot.

Some like it cold,

And some like it hot,

None like it

Nine days old

Sitting in that pot.

34. Pease Porridge Cold

ACTIVITIES FOR SCHOOL

✱ Read the poem aloud. It contains the common word pattern, or word family, *ot*. On chart paper or the board, write the words from the poem that contain this word family: *hot* and *pot*. Read them to the children and, together, brainstorm other words that contain the word family. Record the words and practice reading them with children over the next few days.

✱ Display the poem and help children "voice-point" the lines by
- reading each line two times, pointing at each word as you read, and
- inviting children to read and point along with you.

✱ Display the poem and ask children to find:
- words that contain *o*
- words that end with *t*
- words that begin with *p*

✳ ✳ ✳ ✳

ACTIVITIES FOR HOME

✱ Read the poem aloud. Then, tell your child you're going to clap the syllables, or beats, in each line. Read each line while clapping the syllables. Finally, invite your child to clap along.

✱ After reading the poem, ask your child to listen carefully to the beginning sounds in the following groups of words. Ask him or her to tell you which word in each group has a different beginning sound from the others.
- some, sitting, none
- days, pease, pot

✱ After reading the poem, ask your child to listen carefully to the ending sounds in the following groups of words. Ask him or her to tell you which word in each group has a different ending sound from the others.
- cold, hot, old
- hot, pot, cold

The Lost Shoe

Doodle, doodle, do,

The princess lost her shoe.

Her highness hopped.

The fiddler stopped,

Not knowing what to do.

35. The Lost Shoe

ACTIVITIES FOR SCHOOL

❋ Make a table that looks like this. Put it on the chalkboard or a piece of chart paper. Display the poem and ask children to count the words in each line. Record their totals on the table. Then, clap the syllables in each

Line	Words	"Claps"
1		
2		
3		
4		
5		

line as you reread the poem. Finally, invite children to read and clap along with you. Record the number of "claps" on the table.

❋ Display the poem and the chart and ask children:

- Are there more words or more "claps" in the poem?
- Which two lines have three words?
- Which two lines have four "claps"?

❋ Reread the second line. Point to the words as you read. Next, invite children to read as you point, helping out as needed. Finally, ask children for a word with one "clap" and a word with two "claps." Repeat with lines three and four.

❋ ❋ ❋ ❋ ❋

ACTIVITIES FOR HOME

❋ After reading the poem, ask your child to help you solve these riddles:

- This word sounds like *hop*. We _____ at the _____ sign. (*stop*)
- This word also sounds like *hop*. We do it at the store. (*shop*)
- This word sounds like *do*. It's what we wear on our feet. (*shoe*)
- This word also sounds like *do*. It's the color of the sky on sunny days. (*blue*)

❋ Reread the poem with your child. Ask your child to count the words in each line.

❋ After reading the poem, ask your child:

- Which line starts with *d* ?
- Which two lines end with *d* ?
- Which two lines end with *o* ?
- Which line has three words that all begin with *h* ?

Doodle, Doodle, Dock

Doodle, doodle, dock

The princess lost her sock.

Her highness jumped.

The king was stumped,

While the clock just said,

"Tick tock."

36. Doodle, Doodle, Dock

ACTIVITIES FOR SCHOOL

❋ Make a table that looks like this. Put it on the board or a piece of chart paper. Display the poem and ask children to count the words in each line. Record their totals on the table. Next, clap the syllables in each line as you reread the poem. Then, have children read and clap along with you. Record the number of "claps" on the table.

Line	Words	"Claps"
1		
2		
3		
4		
5		

❋ Display the poem and the chart from the previous activity and ask:
- Which line has the most words? Which line has the fewest words?
- Which line has the most claps?
- Which line has the same number of words and claps?

❋ This poem contains the common word pattern, or word family, *ess*. On chart paper or the board, write these words: *princess* and *highness*. Read them and brainstorm with children other *-ess* words. Record the words and practice reading them.

❋ ❋ ❋ ❋ ❋

ACTIVITIES FOR HOME

❋ After reading the poem, draw your finger under the first line. Ask your child to point to the first word and then the last word in the line. Finally, ask him or her to count the number of words in this line. Repeat with two or three other lines.

❋ Read the poem aloud. It contains the common word pattern, or word family, *ock*. On a blank sheet of paper, write these words from the poem: *dock*, *sock*, and *tock*. Read them to your child and, together, brainstorm other *-ock* words. Write them on the paper and practice reading them with your child over the next few days.

❋ Ask your child to solve the following riddles. Answers will contain the *ock* word family. If answers are on the chart you made with your child, point them out to him or her. If answers are not on the chart, add them.
1. I am another name for a stone. I start with the sound /r/. (*rock*)
2. I am a group of birds flying together. I start with the sound /fl/. (*flock*)
3. I am a place where a boat is tied up. I start with the sound /d/. (*dock*)

Hickory, Dickory Dock

Hickory, dickory dock!

The mouse ran up the clock.

The clock struck one,

And the mouse ran down.

Hickory, dickory dock!

37. Hickory, Dickory Dock

ACTIVITIES FOR SCHOOL

❋ Make several word cards each for *dock* and *clock*. Display the poem, shuffle the cards, and give one to a child. The child should find that word in the poem. Then, shuffle the cards again, and give another card to another child, who should find it in the poem, and so forth.

❋ Play a riddle game with children. Tell them to find answers that rhyme with (sound like) *dock*.

1. To tell time, we look at a _____. (*clock*)

2. Sometimes, a clock says "tick _____." (*tock*)

3. Don't touch a plug or you will get a _____. (*shock*)

4. You can tie up a boat at a _____. (*dock*)

5. An area of houses that has a street on each side is called a _____. (*block*)

❋ Tell children the sound of the letter *k*, /k/. Have them repeat it with you several times. Then say each word below. Ask children whether they hear /k/.

clock	mouse	struck	down	dock	ran

❋ ❋ ❋ ❋

ACTIVITIES FOR HOME

❋ After reading the poem, ask your child:

- Which two lines are the same?
- Which lines have the word *mouse*? (Write this word on a slip of paper for your child.)
- Which lines have the word *dock*? (Write this word on a slip of paper for your child.)
- Which lines have the word *clock*? (Write this word on a slip of paper for your child.)

❋ After reading the poem, show your child the word *the* in line 2 of the poem. Ask your child to find the word *the* elsewhere in the poem.

❋ After reading the poem aloud, write a lowercase *c* on a slip of paper. Show it to your child and name it. Then, ask your child to find words in the poem that have the letter *c*.

The Mouse and the Clock

Dickory, Hickory dock!

The mouse ran up the clock.

The clock cried tick tock,

The mouse was in shock.

Dickory, Hickory dock!

38. The Mouse and the Clock

ACTIVITIES FOR SCHOOL

❋ The poem contains the common word pattern, or word family, *ick*. On chart paper or the board, write *tick*. With the children, brainstorm other words that contain the word family; record them, then practice reading them with the children over the next few days.

❋ Make a two-column chart labeled "-ick" and "-ock." Then, say the following words and ask children to help you decide where to put each word on the chart.

| clock | shock | click | slick | lock | lick | block | tick |

❋ Say these "ick" words. For each one, ask children to say an "ock" word using the same beginning sound.

- *sick* (*sock*)
- *lick* (*lock*)
- *Nick* (*knock*)
- *Rick* (*rock*)

❋ ❋ ❋ ❋ ❋

ACTIVITIES FOR HOME

❋ After reading the poem, draw your finger under the first line. Ask your child to point to the first word and then the last word in this line. Finally, ask your child to count the words in the line. Repeat with two or three other lines.

❋ Read the poem aloud. It contains the common word pattern, or word family, *an*. On a blank sheet of paper, write the word *ran*. Read it to your child and, together, brainstorm other -*an* words. Write the words on the paper and practice reading them with your child over the next few days.

❋ Play a riddle game with your child. Tell your child that answers rhyme with (sound like) *dock*.

1. We look at a _____ to tell time. (*clock*)
2. Tick _____. (*tock*)
3. Before we put on a shoe, we put on a _____. (*sock*)
4. Birds sometimes fly in a _____. (*flock*)
5. We play and build with Legos and _____. (*blocks*)

Pussy Cat

Pussy cat, pussy cat,
Where have you been?
"I've been to London
to visit the queen."

Pussy cat, pussy cat,
What did you there?
"I frightened
a little mouse
under her chair."

39. Pussy Cat

ACTIVITIES FOR SCHOOL

✳ Make several word cards each for *cat* and *you*. Display the poem. Shuffle the cards and give one to a child. The child should find that word in the poem. Shuffle the cards again, give another card to another child, and have the child find it in the poem, and so forth.

✳ Display the poem and ask children to find words that have two of the same letter in them. As they identify words, ask them to name the letter that is used twice.

✳ Ask children to solve these riddles with words that rhyme with (sound like) *there*.

1. This is a piece of furniture for sitting. It starts with /ch/. (*chair*)
2. This is a large animal. It is also a child's toy, a teddy _____. (*bear*)
3. This grows on top of our heads. (*hair*)
4. This means "to look at something without blinking." It starts with /st/. (*stare*)
5. This is a fruit. It starts with /p/. (*pear*)

✳ ✳ ✳ ✳ ✳

ACTIVITIES FOR HOME

✳ After reading the poem, show your child the word *cat* in the title. Ask your child to find the word *cat* in the poem.

✳ Read the poem, then ask your child to find words in the poem that have the letter *s* in them.

✳ After reading the poem, have your child find a word that is in the poem four times. Then ask, "What letter does this word start with?" and "What letter does it end with?" (*Pussy* and *cat* both appear four times.)

Puppy Dog

Puppy dog, puppy dog
Where have you gone?
"I've been to the queen,
who gave me bone."

Puppy dog, puppy dog
What did you see?
"I first saw two cats,
and then I saw three."

40. Puppy Dog

ACTIVITIES FOR SCHOOL

❋ Display the poem and ask children to

- count how many lines there are in the poem.

- find four lines that each have four words.

- find two lines that are the same.

❋ The poem contains the common word pattern, or word family, *ee*. On chart paper or the board, write the words from the poem that contain this word family: *see* and *three*. Read them and then brainstorm other words that contain the word family. Record the words and practice reading them with the children over the next few days.

❋ Say /ee/ several times. Ask children to say it with you. Then say the following words. Ask children to clap or raise their hands each time they hear a word with the /ee/ sound.

| see | sew | tree | trip | bee | back | reel | red | flee | flavor |

* * * * *

ACTIVITIES FOR HOME

❋ Read the poem line by line. After you have read each line, count the words in it, pointing to each word as you count it. Then, read the poem again, pausing at the end of each line to count the words with your child.

❋ Read the poem aloud. It contains the common word pattern, or word family, *og*. On a blank sheet of paper, write the word from the poem that contains this word family: *dog*. Read it to your child and, together, brainstorm other words that contain the word family. Write the words on the paper and practice reading them with your child over the next few days.

❋ Ask your child to solve these riddles. Answers will contain the *og* word family. If the answers are on the chart you made with your child, point them out. If they are not, add them.

1. I am a pet. I start with the sound /d/. (*dog*)

2. I am a long cut-off piece of a tree. I start with the sound /l/. (*log*)

3. I am a very big pig. I start with the sound /h/. (*hog*)

4. I am a small green animal. I live near water. I hop. I start with the sound /fr/. (*frog*)

Banbury Cross

Ride a cock-horse
to Banbury Cross,
to see a fine lady
upon a white horse.
Rings on her fingers
and bells on her toes,
and she shall have music
wherever she goes.

41. Banbury Cross

ACTIVITIES FOR SCHOOL

❋ Display the poem and do voice-pointing with the children. First, read the entire poem, pointing at words as you do. Continue in this way, focusing on lines 2, 3, and 4. Invite children to read along with you as you point at the words. Read and point two or three times with children. Then just point and ask children to read.

❋ Play a riddle game with children. Tell them the answers will rhyme with (sound like) *toes*.

1. During a storm, the wind _____. (*blows*)

2. These are black birds. They start with /kr/. (*crows*)

3. When you turn on a faucet, the water _____ out. (*flows*)

4. My plant _____ when I water it. (*grows*)

❋ Read the poem to children. Read it again, pointing at each word in each line. Ask children to count the words in each line and record totals on a chart like the one shown. Next, clap the syllables in each line, have children count, and record totals on the chart. Ask children some questions, such as "Which line has the most claps?" or "Line three has one more clap than it has words. Can you guess which word has an extra clap?"

Line	Words	"Claps"
1		
2		
3		
4		

❋ ❋ ❋ ❋ ❋

ACTIVITIES FOR HOME

❋ Show your child the word *Banbury* in the title. Ask your child to find the same word in the poem. Repeat with *Cross*.

❋ Say these pairs of words. Ask your child if they rhyme, or sound like each other. Your child may want to raise his or her hand if a pair of words rhymes.

ride, hide	cross, lady	horse, music	goes, toes	bells, tells

❋ After reading the poem, ask your child to find:

• the first line in the poem

• the first word in the poem

• the first word of the second line in the poem

• the last word of the third line in the poem

Ride an Old Car

Ride an old car
and may not get far,
to see a fine lady
in her carriage.
With rings on her fingers
and bells on her toes,
she shall have pretty music
wherever she goes.

42. Ride an Old Car

ACTIVITIES FOR SCHOOL

❋ Display the poem and do voice-pointing with the children. First, read the entire poem, pointing at words as you do. Then, focus on individual lines. Invite children to read along with you as you point at the words. Read and point two or three times with children. Then just point and ask children to read.

❋ This poem contains the common word pattern, or word family, *ar*. On chart paper or the board, write the words from the poem that contain this word family: *far* and *car*. Read them and then brainstorm other words that contain the word family. Record the words and practice reading them with the children over the next few days.

❋ Play a riddle game with the children. Tell the children to find answers that will rhyme with (sound like) *old*.

1. The first line reads, "ride an ___ car." (*old*)
2. If something was bought, it was also ___. (*sold*)
3. The opposite of *hot* is ____. (*cold*).
4. The teacher ___ us to take our seats. (*told*).

❋ ❋ ❋ ❋ ❋

ACTIVITIES FOR HOME

❋ Do an echo reading. First read the poem aloud. Then, reread the first line and have your child repeat it after you. Continue with the rest of the lines.

❋ Say these pairs of words. Ask your child if they rhyme, or sound like each other. Your child may want to raise his or her hand if a pair of words rhymes.

ride, hide	old, ride	car, far	old, cold	car, bells	bells, tells

❋ Say these pairs of words. Ask your child to clap if the words start with the same sound.

ride, rings	car, carriage	far, fine	car, far	lady, music

The Old Woman

The old woman must stand
At the tub, tub, tub,
The dirty clothes
To rub, rub, rub.

But when they are clean
And fit to be seen,
She'll dress like a lady
And dance on the green.

43. The Old Woman

ACTIVITIES FOR SCHOOL

❋ Display the poem and do voice-pointing with the children for lines 2 and 4 of each stanza. First, read the entire poem, pointing at words as you do. Then focus on lines 2 and 4 of the first stanza. Invite children to read along with you as you point at the words. Read and point two or three times with children. Then just point and ask children to read. Repeat with lines 2 and 4 of the second stanza.

❋ Read the poem while clapping the syllables. Then, draw children's attention to the following words. Ask how many "claps" each has:

woman	stand	dirty	clean	lady

❋ Read these pairs of words. Ask children to raise their hands if the words rhyme (sound like each other).

tub, rub	old, dress	stand, band	dance, woman	clean, green

❋ ❋ ❋ ❋ ❋

ACTIVITIES FOR HOME

❋ After reading the poem, write the word *tub* on a slip of paper and show it to your child. Ask your child to find the word in the poem; it appears three times.

❋ Show your child the word *rub*. Ask your child to find three places where the word is used in the poem.

❋ After reading the poem, ask your child to count the words in each line.

Scrubbing the Clothes

The old woman must stand
At the tub, tub, tub,
The dirty clothes
To scrub, scrub, scrub.

But when they are pressed
And she is fit to be dressed,
She'll look like a lady
And not get her
Clothes messed.

44. Scrubbing the Clothes

ACTIVITIES FOR SCHOOL

❋ The poem contains the common word pattern, or word family, *ub*. On chart paper or the board, write the words from the poem that contain this word family: *tub*, *scrub* and *rub*. Read them and then brainstorm other words that contain the word family. Record the words and practice reading them with the children over the next few days.

❋ Ask children to listen to the pairs of words and clap or raise their hands when the words rhyme (sound alike).

stand, band	still, stand	hold, old	rust, must	must, not
	scrub, tub	hot, not		

❋ Ask students to listen carefully to the sounds in the following sets of words. Challenge them to tell which word doesn't belong in each set, and why.

- pressed, messed, dressed, clothes
- tub, not, scrub, rub

❋ ❋ ❋ ❋ ❋

ACTIVITIES FOR HOME

❋ Read the poem aloud. It contains the common word pattern, or word family, *it*. On a blank sheet of paper, write the word from the poem that contains this word family: *fit*. Read it to your child and, together, brainstorm other words that contain the word family. Write the words on the paper and practice reading them with your child over the next few days.

❋ Ask your child to solve the riddles with words that rhyme with (sound like) *dress*.

1. I am something you do with an iron. I start with the sound /pr/. (*press*)
2. I am what you do to answer a riddle. I start with the sound /g/. (*guess*)
3. I am the opposite of *more*. I start with the sound /l/. (*less*)
4. Our new puppy made a _____ when she shredded the newspapers. (*mess*)

❋ Say these words one at a time. Ask your child to clap or raise a hand if the word rhymes with *mess*.

guess	give	Bess	bird	drive	dress

Motion

Fishes swim in water clear,

Birds fly up in the air,

Serpents creep

Along the ground,

Boys and girls run

Round and round.

45. Motion

ACTIVITIES FOR SCHOOL

* Display the poem and do voice-pointing with the children for lines 2 and 4. First, read the entire poem, pointing at words as you do. Then, focus on lines 2 and 4. Invite children to read along with you as you point at the words. Read and point two or three times with children. Then just point and ask children to read.

* Read the poem to children. Then, read it again, pointing at each word in each line. Ask children to count first the words and then the syllables for each line. Record the totals on a chart like the one shown. Ask children some questions, such as "Which line has the most claps?" or "Which two lines have the same number of words as claps?"

Line	Words	"Claps"
1		
2		
3		
4		

* Say each of the following words for children. Ask them to tell how many "claps" each one has:

> swim   water   serpents   creep   ground

* * * * *

ACTIVITIES FOR HOME

* Write the letter *r* on a slip of paper. Then ask your child to find the *r*'s in the poem.
* Say the following pairs of words. Ask your child if they rhyme, or sound like each other. Your child may want to raise his or her hand if a pair of words rhymes.

> clear, near   swim, trim   creep, serpents   ground, round   air, hair

* Put these words on separate slips of paper or index cards: *fishes, swim, birds, fly, serpents, creep.* Shuffle them. Ask your child to put the words in pairs according to what the animals do in the poem; read the cards to your child as he or she works on this activity.

Dogs Run in the Park

Dogs run in the park.

In the ocean

swims the shark.

Serpents creep

along the ground.

Boys and girls run

round and round.

46. Dogs Run in the Park

ACTIVITIES FOR SCHOOL

* On chart paper or the board, write the word from the poem that contains the *un* family: *run*. Read it and then brainstorm other *un* words. Record the words and then practice reading them with the children over the next few days.

* Display the poem and read it aloud. Then read it again, pointing at each word. Ask children to count words and syllables ("claps") for each line. Record totals on a chart like the one shown. Ask children some questions, such as "Which line has the most claps?" or "Which two lines have the same number of words as claps?"

Line	Words	"Claps"
1		
2		
3		
4		

* Say the following pairs of words. Ask children if they rhyme (sound alike). You may ask children to stand, clap, or raise their hands when the pairs rhyme.

| park, dark | park, party | swim, dive | creep, steep | steep, steer | trim, swim |

* * * * *

ACTIVITIES FOR HOME

* Read the poem. Then, read the first line again, this time clapping the syllables, or beats, in each word. Finally, invite your child to clap along with you. Repeat for each line, for as long as your child is interested.

* Ask your child to find the *n*'s in the poem. Repeat with *t* and *r*. (If your child does not know what the letters look like, write them on a slip of paper first.)

* Play a riddle game with your child. Tell your child to find answers that will rhyme with (sound like) *ground*.

  1. The shape of a ball is _____. (*round*)
  2. The opposite of *lost* is _____. (*found*)
  3. When you hear something, you hear a ____.(*sound*)
  4. A big pile of dirt creates a _____. (*mound*)

Bees

A swarm of bees in May

Is worth a load of hay.

A swarm of bees in June

Is worth a silver spoon.

A swarm of bees in July

Is not worth a fly.

47. Bees

ACTIVITIES FOR SCHOOL

✳ Display the poem and do voice-pointing with the children for lines 3 and 5. First, read the entire poem, pointing at words as you do. Then focus on lines 3 and 5. Invite children to read along with you as you point at the words. Read and point two or three times with children. Then just point and ask children to read.

✳ Say each of the following words for children. Ask them to tell how many "claps" each one has:

bees	load	silver	July	fly

✳ Play a riddle game with children. Tell them that the answers will rhyme with (sound like) *May*.

1. At recess, I like to _____ games. (*play*)
2. I taught my dog to sit and _____. (*stay*)
3. One _____ has 24 hours. (*day*)
4. This is a color. It's between white and black. It starts with /gr/. (*gray*)
5. This means "to move back and forth." It starts with /sw/. (*sway*)

✳ ✳ ✳ ✳ ✳

ACTIVITIES FOR HOME

✳ Read the poem through once. Then, reread the first line and count the words in it. Repeat for each line in the poem. When you have finished, invite your child to read each line with you and to count the words in each line.

✳ Read one line of the poem three times. First, just read it through. Next, read it while pointing to each word. Finally, ask your child to point as you read. Repeat with other lines, if your child remains interested.

✳ After reading the poem, write *bees* on a slip of paper and show the word to your child. Ask your child to find this word in the poem.

Bees in the Summer

A swarm of bees in the summer
Can be a bummer.
A swarm of bees in the fall
Can be a ball.
A swarm of bees in the winter
Can be like a splinter.
A swarm of bees in the spring?
You can hear them sing.

Fast Start: Getting Ready to Read

48. Bees in the Summer

ACTIVITIES FOR SCHOOL

✳ Display and do voice-pointing with the children for lines 3, 5, and 7. First, read the entire poem, pointing at words as you do. Then, focus on lines 3, 5, and 7. Invite children to read along with you as you point at the words. Read and point two or three times with children. Then just point and ask children to read.

✳ The poem contains the common word pattern, or word family, *all*. On chart paper or the board, write the words from the poem that contain this word family: *fall* and *ball*. Read them and, together with the children, brainstorm other words that contain the word family. Record the words and practice reading them with the children over the next few days.

✳ Say the following words one at a time. Ask children to tell you how many claps the word has by putting that many fingers in the air.

swarm	bees	summer	fall	can	ball	splinter
		winter	spring	sing		

✳ ✳ ✳ ✳ ✳

ACTIVITIES FOR HOME

✳ After reading the poem, ask your child to count the words in each line.

✳ Read the poem aloud. It contains the common word pattern, or word family, *ing*. On a blank sheet of paper, write the words from the poem that contain this word family: *spring* and *sing*. Read them to your child and, together, brainstorm other words that contain the word family. Write the words on the paper and practice reading them with your child over the next few days.

✳ After reading the poem, ask your child to listen carefully to the sounds in each group of words and to tell you which word doesn't belong. Note there are two ways to solve groups 1, 2, and 4.

- fall, bees, ball
- fan, fort, can
- bird, wing, spring
- bees, birds, knees

Three Little Kittens

Three little kittens lost their mittens,

And they began to cry:

"Oh Mother, dear, we greatly fear

That we have lost our mittens!"

"Lost your mittens?

You naughty kittens.

Then you shall have no pie."

"Mee-ow, mee-ow, mee-ow!

And we can have no pie.

Mee-ow, mee-ow, mee-ow!"

49. Three Little Kittens

ACTIVITIES FOR SCHOOL

❋ Display the poem and read it aloud. Then read it again, pointing at each word in each line. Ask children to count words and syllables ("claps") in each line. Record totals on a chart similar to the one at right. Ask children some questions, such as "Which line has the most claps?" "Which line has the fewest claps?"

Line	Words	"Claps"
1		
2		
3		
4		

❋ Tell children you are going to say some words very slowly, like a turtle. Their job is to tell you what the words are:

three	they	little	lost	mittens	mother

❋ Say each of the following words for children. Ask them to tell how many "claps" each one has:

three	they	little	lost	mother	mittens

❋ ❋ ❋ ❋

ACTIVITIES FOR HOME

❋ After reading the poem, say the following pairs of words. Ask your child to tell you if the words start the same. (You may want to exaggerate the beginning sounds.)

mother, mittens	little, lost	kittens, pie	we, you	naughty, nice

❋ Reread the second stanza of the poem. Ask your child to say the "Mee-ow, mee-ow, mee-ow!" lines and to try to sound like a sad kitten.

❋ Looking at just the first four lines, ask your child to
  • find three words that start with *m*.
  • find three words that start with *th*.
  • find four words with *tt* in the middle.
  • find three words that end in *r*.

Cats and Their Hats

Three little cats lost their hats
And they began to shake:
"Oh Mother, dear, we greatly fear
That we have lost our hats."

"Lost your hats? You naughty cats.
Then you shall have no cake."
"Mee-ow, mee-ow, mee-ow!
And we can have no cake.
Mee-ow, mee-ow, mee-ow!"

50. Cats and Their Hats

ACTIVITIES FOR SCHOOL

✳ Read the poem aloud. Then, read the poem again while clapping the syllables. Finally, invite children to clap along with you. Repeat if children's interest is sustained.

✳ Play a riddle game with the children. Tell the children to find answers that will rhyme with (sound like) *bake*.

1. In the rhyme, the cats want a piece of _____ . (*cake*)

2. You ___ a picture with crayons. (*make*)

3. If something is not real, it's _____ . (*fake*)

✳ Say the following words, one at a time. Ask children to think about how many claps the word has and to put that many fingers in the air for each.

lost	naughty	hats	little	cats	fear	shake

✳ ✳ ✳ ✳ ✳

ACTIVITIES FOR HOME

✳ Do an echo reading. First, read the poem aloud. Then, reread the first line and have your child repeat it after you. Continue with the rest of the lines.

✳ Read the poem aloud. It contains the common word pattern, or word family, *at*. On a blank sheet of paper, write the words from the poem that contain this word family: *cat* and *hat*. Read them to your child and, together, brainstorm other words that contain the word family. Write the words on the paper and practice reading them with your child over the next few days.

✳ After reading the poem, say these pairs of words. Ask your child to tell you if they rhyme (or sound alike). Your child could do "thumbs up" for pairs that rhyme and "thumbs down" for pairs that don't.

mother, father	cry, pie	frost, lost	dear, daddy	dear, fear	see, we

Peter Piper

Peter Piper picked a peck
of pickled peppers.
A peck of pickled peppers
Peter Piper picked.
If Peter Piper picked a peck
of pickled peppers,
where's the peck of pickled
peppers Peter Piper picked?

51. Peter Piper

ACTIVITIES FOR SCHOOL

* Display the poem and ask children to count the number of words that begin with *p* in each line.

* Display the poem and ask children to count the total number of *p*'s in each line.

* Write the following words on chart paper or the board. Display the poem and invite children to find the words in the poem.

Peter	Piper	peck	picked	peppers

* * * * *

ACTIVITIES FOR HOME

* This is a tongue twister. Try reading each line several times along with your child. Each time you read it, try to go faster. See how quickly you can read the lines without twisting your tongues!

* After reading the poem, ask your child to underline all the *p*'s in the poem. If necessary, help your child do this.

* After reading the poem, ask your child to tell you the letters that begin and end each line.

Busy Billy

Busy Billy bought

a bushel of blueberries.

A bushel of blueberries

busy Billy did buy.

If busy Billy bought

a bushel of blueberries,

where's the bushel

of blueberries

busy Billy bought?

52. Busy Billy

ACTIVITIES FOR SCHOOL

✳ Write the following words on chart paper or the board. Display the poem and invite children to find the words in the poem.

Billy	busy	buy	bushel

✳ Write an uppercase and a lowercase *b* on the board or chart paper. Display the poem and ask children to count all the *b*'s in the poem, line by line.

✳ Make a two-column chart labeled "One Clap" and "Two Claps." Then, say the following words. Have the children repeat them and clap the beats; then children can help you put them in the correct column on the chart.

busy	Billy	bought	bushel	buy

✳ ✳ ✳ ✳ ✳

ACTIVITIES FOR HOME

✳ Do an echo reading. First, read the poem aloud. Then, reread the first line and have your child repeat it after you. Continue with the rest of the lines.

✳ This is a tongue twister. Try reading each line several times along with your child. Each time you read it, try to go faster. See how quickly you can read the lines without twisting your tongues!

✳ After reading the poem, ask your child to circle the words that begin with *b*. Then, ask your child what sound he or she hears at the beginning of *busy* and *Billy*.

As I Was Going Along

As I was going along, along,

a-singing a comical

song, song, song,

the lane where I went was so

long, long, long,

and the song that I sang was so

long, long, long,

and so I went singing along.

53. As I Was Going Along

ACTIVITIES FOR SCHOOL

❋ Display the poem and ask children:

- how many times is the word *along* used in line 1? Where are these words?
- how many times is the word *song* used in line 3? Where are these words?
- how many times is the word *long* used in lines 5 and 7 together? Where are these words?

❋ Make a chart like the one below:

A only	O only	A and O

Then, show the following words to children. Ask them to look carefully at the letters in each word and decide where the words belong on the chart.

as	along	comical	song	long

❋ Read the poem while pointing to the words. Ask children to count words per line. (They have already done this on several occasions. See if they can do it now independently. If not, provide assistance.) Then, read the poem and clap the syllables. Ask children to try this independently (provide assistance if needed).

❋ ❋ ❋ ❋ ❋

ACTIVITIES FOR HOME

❋ After reading the poem, write the word *song* on a slip of paper and show it to your child. Ask your child to find the word three times in the poem. Repeat for *long* (which appears six times) and *along* (which appears three times).

❋ Read the poem aloud. Then, tell your child you're going to clap the syllables, or beats, in each line. Read each line while clapping the syllables. Finally, invite your child to clap along.

❋ Read the poem line by line. After you have read each line, count the words in it, pointing to each word as you count it. Then, read the poem again, pausing at the end of each line to count the words with your child.

Walking and Talking

As I was walking

along, along

I was talking to my friend so

strong, strong, strong.

The road where we walked was so

long, long, long,

I saw the way we were going was

wrong, wrong, wrong.

54. Walking and Talking

ACTIVITIES FOR SCHOOL

❋ The poem contains the common word pattern, or word family, *ong*. On chart paper or the board, write the words from the poem that contain this word family: *along, wrong, long,* and *strong*. Read them and then brainstorm with the children other words that contain the word family. Record the words and practice reading them with the children over the next few days.

❋ Ask children to help you fill in the blanks with words from the *ong* family.

1. My favorite _____ is "Happy Birthday to You." (*song*)
2. The opposite of *short* is _____. (*long*)
3. I like jelly _____ with peanut butter on my sandwiches. (*along*)
4. The bell says ding _____ when it rings. (*dong*)
5. The opposite of *right* is _____. (*wrong*)

❋ Ask students to listen carefully to the sounds in the words and to figure out which one doesn't belong.

- long, song, talk
- plane, lane, walk
- talk, sing, chalk
- bent, Bobby, sent [note the two ways to solve this one]

❋ ❋ ❋ ❋ ❋

ACTIVITIES FOR HOME

❋ After reading the poem, count the words in the first line. Then, ask your child to count the words by himself or herself. Help out if needed. Repeat with lines 2, 3, and 4.

❋ Read the poem, then write "ong" on a small piece of paper. Show it to your child and ask him or her to circle all the words containing the word family *ong*.

❋ After reading the poem, say each pair of words listed below. Tell your child to make a funny face if the pair rhymes (sounds alike).

- went, sent
- walk, wet
- talk, walk
- song, bang
- lane, mane
- little, lane

Old Mother Hubbard

Old Mother Hubbard

Went to the cupboard

To get her poor dog a bone.

When she got there,

The cupboard was bare,

And so the poor dog had none.

55. Old Mother Hubbard

ACTIVITIES FOR SCHOOL

✳ Read the poem aloud. Then tell children you're going to clap the syllables in each line. Read the poem again while clapping the syllables. Finally, invite children to clap along with you. Repeat if children's interest is sustained.

✳ Tell children you are going to talk like a turtle and that they need to figure out what words you are saying. Say each of these words slowly, stretching out the sounds in an exaggerated manner:

mother	poor	she	old	her

✳ Make a three-column chart labeled "Beginning," "Middle," and "End." Display the poem and show children the following words. For each, ask where the *o* is in the word. Put the words in the appropriate place on the chart:

poor	dog	old	so	to

✳ ✳ ✳ ✳ ✳

ACTIVITIES FOR HOME

✳ After reading the poem, ask your child to find:
  • a word that starts with *o*
  • two words that end with *o*
  • two words that have *o* in the middle

✳ After reading the poem, ask your child to find:
  • two words that have two letters
  • three words that have three letters
  • four words that have four letters

✳ After reading the poem, ask your child to find words that contain these letters: *a, b, c, d, e.*

No Treats!

Old Mother Hubbard

Went to the cupboard

To get her poor dog a treat.

When she got there,

The cupboard was bare,

And so the poor dog had

Nothing to eat.

56. No Treats!

ACTIVITIES FOR SCHOOL

* Do an echo reading. First, read the poem aloud. Then, reread the first line and have children repeat it after you. Continue with the rest of the lines.

* Say the following rhyming word pairs. Ask children to brainstorm other words that rhyme with each pair:

there, bare	treat, eat

* Display the poem. Ask children to point to the longest line and count the words in it. Then, ask them to point to the shortest line and count the words in it. Finally, ask them to find the longest and shortest words, and count the letters in each.

✳ ✳ ✳ ✳ ✳

ACTIVITIES FOR HOME

* Read the poem line by line. After you have read each line, count the words in it, pointing to each word as you count it. Then, read the poem again, pausing at the end of each line to count the words with your child.

* The poem contains the common word pattern, or word family, *eat*. On a blank sheet of paper, write the words from the poem that contain this word family: *eat* and *treat*. Read them to your child and, together, brainstorm other words that contain the word family. Write the words on the paper and practice reading them with your child over the next few days.

* After reading the poem, play a word game with your child. Ask your child to answer the riddles with words that rhyme with (sound like) *eat*.
  1. The teacher said, "Take your _____." (*seat*)
  2. Dad stopped by the butcher shop to buy _____ for dinner. (*meat*)
  3. My room is messy, but my sister's is _____. (*neat*)
  4. A _____ on my left soccer shoe snapped off. (*cleat*)

Simple Simon

Simple Simon met a pieman
Going to the fair.
Said Simple Simon to the pieman,
"Let me taste your ware."

Said the pieman to Simple Simon,
"Show me first your penny."
Said Simple Simon to the pieman,
"Alas, I have not any."

57. Simple Simon

ACTIVITIES FOR SCHOOL

✳ Ask children to tell you how many "claps," or syllables, are in each of these words:

fair	going	simple	have	any

✳ Make a two-column chart labeled "One Clap" and "Two Claps." Display the poem and read each word in the first stanza. Ask children to help you decide where each word goes on the chart.

✳ Ask children to provide a rhyming word for each of the following. Invite children to think of as many words as possible. Write them on the chalkboard or chart paper. Then, help children see that sometimes words sound alike but are spelled differently:

fair	met	said	to	taste

✳ ✳ ✳ ✳ ✳

ACTIVITIES FOR HOME

✳ After reading the poem, show your child the word *Simple* in the title of the poem. Ask your child to find this word in the poem. Repeat with *Simon*.

✳ Read the poem, then ask your child to find *p*'s in the words of the poem.

✳ After reading the poem, say these pairs of words. Ask your child to tell you if the words rhyme (sound alike). If the words do rhyme, ask your child if he or she can provide a third word that also rhymes.

fair, ware	said, red	me, tree	penny, have	let, get

Caring Carrie

Caring Carrie met a baker

Going to the lake.

Said caring Carrie to the baker,

"Let me taste your cake."

Said the baker to caring Carrie,

"Show me your dollar one."

Said caring Carrie to the baker,

"Alas, I have none."

58. Caring Carrie

ACTIVITIES FOR SCHOOL

✻ The poem contains the common word pattern, or word family, *ake*. On chart paper or the board, write the words from the poem that contain this word family: *lake* and *cake*. Read them and then brainstorm other words that contain the word family. Record the words and practice reading them with the children over the next few days.

✻ Say each of these words. Elongate the sound of *a* in each word. Ask children to listen for the letter *a* (i.e., for the long sound of *a*, say, "Do you hear /ā/ in these words?"). Children may want to raise their hands or clap if they hear the long sound of *a*:

| lake | baker | taste | alas | have | said |

✻ Ask students to listen carefully to the sounds in the words and to tell you which one doesn't belong.
  • cake, bake, lake, walk
  • one, dollar, none
  • waste, water, taste (note 2 possible answers)

✻ ✻ ✻ ✻ ✻

ACTIVITIES FOR HOME

✻ After reading the poem, draw your finger under the first line. Say to your child, "Point at the first word in this line. What letter starts this word? What letter ends it?" Then say, "Point to the last word in this line. What letter starts this word? What letter ends it?" Repeat with two or three other lines.

✻ After reading the poem, say each pair of words. Tell your child to make a silly face if the words rhyme (sound alike).

| one, none | cake, bake | cake, walk | caring, daring | caring, carrying |

✻ Say each pair of words. Tell your child to raise his or her hand if the words begin with the same sound.

| caring, Carrie | bake, cake | lake, let | taste, to | dollar, one |

There Was an Old Woman

There was an old woman
tossed up in a blanket
seventy times
as high as the moon.
What she did there,
I cannot tell you,
but in her hand she carried a broom.

"Old woman, old woman, old woman,"
said I.
"O whither, o whither, o whither
so high?"
"To sweep the cobwebs from the sky.
And I shall be back again,
by and by."

Fast Start: Getting Ready to Read

59. There Was an Old Woman

ACTIVITIES FOR SCHOOL

❋ Ask children to provide a rhyming word for each of the following words. Invite them to think of as many words as possible. Write the word on the board or chart paper. Then, help children see that sometimes words sound alike but are spelled differently:

old	high	back	hand	sweep

❋ Ask children to tell you how many "claps," or syllables, are in each word.

woman	blanket	moon	cobwebs	sky	again

❋ Make a two-column chart labeled "One Clap" and "Two Claps." Display the poem and read each word in the first stanza. Ask children to help you decide where each word goes on the chart.

❋ ❋ ❋ ❋ ❋

ACTIVITIES FOR HOME

❋ After reading the poem, say to your child:
  • Put your finger on the first word in the poem. (*There*)
  • Put your finger on the last word in the poem. (*by*)
  • How many words are in the first line in the poem? (five)
  • How many words are in the last line of the poem? (three)

❋ Give your child a pencil or crayon and ask him or her to draw a line between two words, separating them. Then, ask your child to select a line from the poem and separate all the words from each other by drawing lines between them.

❋ After reading the poem, ask your child to find all the *a*'s in the poem.

She Carried a Mop

There was an old woman
tossed up in a blanket
seventy times as high as the treetop.
What she did there, I cannot tell you,
but in her hand she carried a mop.

"Old woman, old woman, old woman,"
said I.
"O whither, o whither, o whither
so high?"
"To wash the cobwebs while in flight.
And I shall be back again,
at night at night."

60. She Carried a Mop

ACTIVITIES FOR SCHOOL

✳ Ask children to provide a rhyming word for each of the following words. Invite them to think of as many words as possible. Write the words on the board or chart paper. Then, help children see that sometimes words sound alike but are spelled differently:

old	top	tell	high	back	night

✳ The poem contains the common word pattern, or word family, *ight*. On chart paper or the board, write the *ight* words from the poem: *flight* and *night*. Read them and then brainstorm other words that contain the word family. Record the words and practice reading them with the children over the next few days.

✳ Play a riddle game with the children. Tell the children that answers will rhyme with (sound like) *flight*.

1. The moon comes out at _____. (*night*)
2. When there are no clouds in the sky, the sun is _____. (*bright*)
3. The opposite of *heavy* is _____. (*light*)
4. The sense of _____ involves our eyes. (*sight*)
5. On windy days, we can fly a _____. (*kite*)

✳ ✳ ✳ ✳ ✳

ACTIVITIES FOR HOME

✳ After reading the poem, draw your finger under the first line. Say to your child, "Point to the first word in this line. What letter starts this word? What letter ends it?" Then say, "Point to the last word in this line. What letter starts this word? What letter ends it?" Repeat with two or three other lines.

✳ Give your child a pencil or crayon and ask him or her to draw a line in the space between two words, separating them. Then, ask your child to select a line from the poem and separate all the words from each other by drawing lines between them.

✳ After reading the following words, ask your child to tell you the opposite of each word. Write the word pairs on a piece of paper.

old	top	high	back	night

References & Resources for Further Learning

Chavkin, N. F. (Ed.). (1993). *Families and schools in a pluralistic society*. Albany, NY: State University of New York Press.

Durkin, D. (1966). *Children who read early*. New York: Teachers College Press.

Epstein, J. L. (1989). Family structures and student motivation: A developmental perspective. In C. Ames & R. Ames (Eds.), *Research on motivation in education: Vol. 3., Goals and cognitions* (pp. 259–295). New York: Academic Press.

Epstein, J. L. (1991). Effect on student achievement of teacher's practices of parent involvement. In *Advances in reading/language research: Literacy through family, community and school interaction* (Vol. 5, pp. 261–276). Greenwich, CT: JAI Press.

Henderson, A. (1988). Parents are a school's best friends. *Phi Delta Kappan, 70*, 148–153.

Henderson, A., & Berla, N. (Eds.). (1994). *A new generation of evidence: The family is critical to student achievement*. Washington, DC: National Committee for Citizens in Education.

Neidermeyer, F. C. (1970). Parents teach kindergartners at home. *The Elementary School Journal, 70*, 439–445.

Padak, N., & Rasinski, T. (2004). Fast Start: A promising practice for family literacy programs. *Family Literacy Forum, 3*(2), 3–9.

Padak, N., & Rasinski, T. (2006). Home-school partnerships in literacy education: From rhetoric to reality. *The Reading Teacher, 60*, 292–295.

Postlethwaite, T. N., & Ross, K. N. (1992). *Effective schools in reading: Implications for policy planners*. The Hague: International Association for the Evaluation of Educational Achievement.

Pressley, M. (2002). Effective beginning reading instruction. *Journal of Literacy Research, 34*, 165–188.

Rasinski, T. V. (1989). Reading and empowerment of parents. *The Reading Teacher, 34*, 226–231.

Rasinski, T. V. (1995). Fast Start: A parental involvement reading program for primary grade children. In W. Linek & E. Sturtevant (Eds.), *Generations of literacy: Seventeenth yearbook of the College Reading Association* (pp. 301–312). Harrisonburg, VA: College Reading Association.

Rasinski, T. V. (2003). Parental involvement: Key to leaving no child behind in reading. *The New England Reading Association Journal, 39*, 1–5.

Rasinski, T., & Hoffman, J. (2003). Oral reading and the school literacy curriculum. *Reading Research Quarterly, 38*, 510–522.

Rasinski, T., & Stevenson, B. (2005). The effects of Fast Start Reading, a fluency based home involvement reading program, on the reading achievement of beginning readers. *Reading Psychology: An International Quarterly, 26*, 109–125.

U. S. Department of Education. (1994). *Strong families, strong schools: Building community partnerships for learning*. Washington, DC.